Websites
for
Small Business

Good Advice
in Plain English
for the
Small Business Owner

By Marianne Carlson

For my crazy, dysfunctional, wonderful family,
with love.

ISBN 978-0-557-15624-5

Table of Contents

Foreword

Like many professionals who decide to start their own business, I was an expert in my field and I knew, from a technical standpoint, exactly how I wanted to operate, my safety consulting business. But the nuts and bolts of establishing and operating a business were all new to me, and I had to rely on business advisors for my start-up. I knew I needed a website and I learned from a mutual friend that one of our former colleagues had recently started a business and their website was awesome. I visited their website and I loved it. When I called Don for information about how to get a website like his, I learned that Marianne had built the site for their family business. I knew then that I had found my website designer.

I have known Marianne Carlson for many years and she has always been motivated to complete assignments with attention to detail, promptness of schedule, and personal integrity. When I learned of her IT experience culminating in a six month assignment to Iraq and her website design experience at West Point, it was clear that she had built a strong foundation based on technical knowledge and practical application of her skills. I suggested that she could build a website for me as a part of their existing business, however, Marianne had already been thinking about starting a graphic design business because of the satisfaction she gets from building websites and the rave reviews she had received for her existing work. At that point, she decided to proceed with the new business and Emcie Graphic Design LLC was born.

Marianne explained the website process thoroughly before we began, going into detail about the purpose of the site, the image to be presented and content to be provided. I didn't know much about web design or hosting, so I was grateful for her advice and patience as we worked through the details. She even helped me select an appropriate hosting service. As she was building my website, she kept me informed of the progress every step of the way. When the site was completed, she delivered a package containing all of the information used to build the website, including contact information and passwords necessary to update the site.

Since launching the website, I have used Marianne to design business forms that are consistent with the look and feel of my website. She has also prepared sales and marketing documents using both digital and printed media. My power point presentations have an attractive visual appearance and a concise written message that conveys the image that I want to present to my current and potential clients. The powerful combination of my website and the supporting promotional material provides the perfect accent for my corporate image.

I can't say enough about how valuable it has been to my business to work with Marianne. The service she provides to me and her other clients, and the information available to her business associates is a great resource for those in her network. Now that she has written *Websites for Small Business: Good Advice in Plain English for the Small Business Owner*, the basic information about the process required for anyone to build, launch, and maintain a website is available to everyone. Every business needs a web presence to communicate their message to their desired audience. While the message may vary and the target audience may differ, this book provides essential information to the business community.

William Loeser
President
L2 Solutions, LLC

Part I

Introduction

CHAPTER 1

About This Book

*W*ebsites for Small Business was written for anyone who owns, manages or makes decisions for a small business in America, and for anyone who is contemplating starting a new business. If you are a business owner, or hope one day to be one, this book was written for you.

You are not a complete idiot, or even a dummy. You are an entrepreneur – an intelligent individual with a passion for your business. You are an expert in your own chosen field. But chances are, you are not an expert in computer technology. So *Websites for Small Business* is written in plain English, without any baffling technical jargon.

Whether you are about to tiptoe for the first time into the world of websites, or you already have a website that isn't performing the way you'd like it to, this book will help you save time, money and aggravation. As a small business owner myself, I know how precious your time and money are. So I've written this book to give you some good, honest advice about website ownership. Armed with the information in this book, you'll be able to make better decisions, negotiate better deals, and develop a better website for your business.

How you use this book will depend on your own level of expertise. As you glance through the table of contents, you may find you are already knowledgeable in some areas. If that's the case, feel free to skip around. Look for the topics you are especially interested in and grab the information you need.

But if you are a relative novice in the world of website design, I encourage you to read the book cover to cover. In fact, the book is organized with the novice in mind. Beginning with the basics and building on that foundation, each chapter will provide a deeper understanding and further detail about the issues and components of website ownership.

As painless as possible

Websites for Small Business is really a very easy read. I've presented the topics in a logical order, and kept the language simple and straightforward. There's a Glossary of Terms in the back of the book, in case you forget something we discussed in a previous chapter. And I've used a few visual tools like illustrations and text boxes to make the learning easier and more fun.

How this book is organized

In the beginning…

In the early chapters, I assume you know nothing – or very little – about computers and websites. I start with the basics and explain all the jargon. This is great for you because it removes the mystery and empowers you. Once you understand the basics, you'll know enough to speak with a web designer or developer without being intimidated. As you read through the remaining chapters, you'll come to appreciate how very powerful a little knowledge can be.

Who will build it?

As you develop a website plan, you will have options all along the way. But the process begins with answering one fundamental question: "Who is gong to build this website?" We'll discuss the options, the pros and cons, and help you make a decision that is right for your situation and your business.

Let the games begin!

Once you know the basics of website ownership, and you've decided who will build your site, I'll take you through the remaining topics. You'll learn about how to choose a good designer for your particular business, what it should cost, how to keep it updated, and how to get help when you need it. You'll learn how to choose a good hosting service for your site and how much it should cost. And you'll learn some very important tips to assure that you are always in control of your website, no matter who builds it or how it is maintained.

And in closing...

In the back of the book, I provide you with a Glossary of Terms so you can look up some quick definitions or jog your memory about a specific topic. And there's a short biographical piece called About the Author. I've actually led a pretty interesting life, so you might well enjoy reading that.

A word about gender:

Throughout this book, I refer to web designers, clients, visitors, and business owners using the male pronoun. I have chosen to ignore gender entirely simply because I have found that it makes for easier reading.

Like many readers, I am annoyed by the tedious attempts to be politically correct in the use of gender. I believe that using "he or she" in a sentence detracts from its clarity. And I find that using "he" in one paragraph and "she" in the next is distracting at best.

This is a book about a serious and complex topic, and I am trying to make it easy and enjoyable to read and understand. By using the male pronouns, I don't intend to suggest anything untoward about the female segment of the population. In fact, I myself am a female web designer, client, visitor, and business owner. I am simply trying to reach my readers with the clearest and most understandable language possible.

Should anyone be offended by this, I encourage him to get over it.

CHAPTER 2

The Basics

Before we can have a meaningful discussion about your website, it will be helpful to set down a few basic definitions so there are no misunderstandings going forward. These words will be used repeatedly throughout the book, so it's important we all have a unified idea about what they mean. Let's start with the obvious

What is a Website?

Yes, you probably know what a website is, and I don't mean to insult your intelligence. But there are two ways of looking at a website, so you need to understand both of them.

From a visitor's viewpoint, a website is a place on the *World Wide Web* (also known as the *Internet*). There are lots of different kinds of websites – They are as varied as the people who build them and the businesses the represent. Most websites provide visual information - text, pictures, graphs, and the like.

And many provide audio information as well. Some play music; others play videos. If you have spent time on the web, you know how varied websites can be.

From a business owner's viewpoint, a website is a little different. When we talk about YOUR website, we're not just talking about a place on the web, we're talking about all the components that make up the website your visitors see. The files, the text, the pictures, the colors, the buttons, the sounds, the links, everything.

> If you have never spent time on the web, put down this book and get to a computer. Find a 12-year-old to help you (or a volunteer at your local library), and familiarize yourself with the greatest invention in modern history. The rest of this book assumes you have at least a general familiarity with the Internet. So once you've got that, come on back. Go ahead. We'll wait.

What is Hosting?

Imagine for a moment that I am a *web designer* - a person who creates websites for a living. (I actually am a web designer, so it's not too big of a stretch.) When I build a website, I take all my client's words and pictures and I build a website on my computer. I create the files and the links and the buttons, and I make it all work to produce a beautiful website. But people around the world can't access that website while it's sitting on my computer, and that's a problem.

In order for the public to be able to see that website, I have to move those files from my computer onto a special computer, called a *web server*, that people around the world can access. We say that the web server "*hosts*" that website. As a website owner, you will pay a Hosting Service or Hosting Provider a monthly fee for the use of their web server. And they will maintain the server and keep it running 24/7/365 so your website is available to anyone on the Internet. Once your website is stored on the web server, it will remain there as long as you pay your hosting charges, and keep your domain registration current.

What is a Domain?

Your domain is the spot on the Internet reserved for your website. And your Domain Name is your website's name on the Internet. For most American businesses, it usually ends with ".com" or ".net". For example, my web design business has a website, and its domain name is "emcie.com".

The important thing to know about Domain Names is that it *must be unique*. There can be only one "emcie.com" in the entire world, so you'll need to choose a domain name that hasn't already been taken by someone else.

You can search for an available name on the website of a domain registrar. GoDaddy and Network Solutions are two of the largest ones, and they can tell you if the name you want is available, and suggest similar alternatives if it isn't.

Your domain also includes your email addresses (like "theboss@emcie.com"), so keeping the name short has real advantages.

What is website maintenance?

This term is often confused with hosting, but maintenance is very different from hosting. Remember that a hosting service provides space on their web server for your website files. Web maintenance involves updates and re-designs of your website in order to keep its content current, relevant and up-to-date.

If your website includes a shopping cart, adding new products and changing prices are part of your web maintenance. If your site includes a newsletter that needs to be updated every month, that also falls under web maintenance.

What is E-Commerce?

Simply put, e-commerce is the ability of a website to handle online transactions, accept payments, or manage inventories. If you plan to sell items online, (using a shopping cart, for example), or you want to accept credit card payments through your website, you'll need an e-commerce website.

CHAPTER 3

Who Should Build Your Site

You have decided you need a website, or maybe you have one that needs updated. So who should you get to build it? The short and ideal answer to this question is, "A professional web designer or web developer should build your site", but in the real world there are financial reasons for considering other options. There are three common options available to you:

1. I will build it myself.
2. I have a friend will build it for free.
3. I will pay a professional to build it.

Let's take these options one at a time and discuss the pros and cons.

Option 1: You can build it yourself. Or have someone within your organization build it for you. There are a few very good reasons to consider this option, not the least of which is money. If cash flow is a serious consideration, you can save money by taking on the job yourself. And if you are just starting out and have a lot of free time, it might be the way to go. You'll pay for a domain name and a hosting package, but you'll probably save a few hundred in design charges.

Another good reason to do it yourself is because you know what you want it to look like, and you don't feel comfortable delegating the design to someone else. If you are an accomplished designer, or have at least a practiced talent in visual design, you might well want to design it yourself. But most build-it-yourself programs are built using templates that are not as easy to customize as they may seem at first. It's not unusual for a business owner to spend many hours just trying to get their logo inserted into a template. Again, this is only a good option if you have lots of free time.

If you plan to build a very simple site – three or four pages a few pictures, and some text, and if you have plenty of free time to handle the frustrations and tedium involved in customizing a template, then building your own site can be a viable alternative for you. Sites like GoDaddy.com and NetworkSolutions.com offer packages that allow a novice to build his own website from a template. And most of those sites offer technical assistance for those times when you really get stuck. Be aware, however, that most of these templates offer very little flexibility. You will probably be limited in the number of pages, the number of email accounts, and the amount of data you can store on the site. You may also find that the design itself is very rigid, so that images, headings, and fonts have to be a set size in order to work in the template.

The ads may say the templates are easy to customize, but that has not been my experience. While replacing a paragraph of text with your own paragraph of text may be simple enough, I have found many templates that make replacing images practically impossible.

You'll need to edit your photos so they fit neatly in the space allocated by the template, and so they load quickly onto your website. Otherwise, your visitors will get tired of waiting and move on to someone else's website. Optimizing photos for use on the web isn't difficult if you have the right software (Adobe Photoshop, for example). There are some free software packages available on the Internet to help you optimize your images, but I can't personally recommend any of them. Nor can I be certain those will still exist by the time this book winds up in your hands. My best advice for those is to do a Google search for "free photo optimizing" and see what turns up.

If you have the software and knowledge to build a site from the ground up (as opposed to using a template), you'll have much more flexibility and control. And if you also have the skill to design an appealing and functional layout, you might be a candidate for building your site yourself. Then it's just a question of time. If you have lots of time to devote to your website, you might well be able to save the expense of hiring it done. But even a very simple site can easily take a novice 30-40 hours to create. If you time is worth anything, I strongly recommend you look for a better solution.

A final caveat: When you build a website using a build-it-yourself template package like those described above, the hosting provider usually maintains ownership of the site. You will own your domain name, but they will maintain ownership of the design. (In essence, you'll be leasing the site.) If you decide to take your site elsewhere in the future, or if you want it redesigned to incorporate additional features, you probably won't be able to do that. In that case, you'll have to purchase a different hosting plan – one that allows you to build you pages on your own computer and upload your new web pages to the web server.

Option 2: You have a friend, neighbor, or family member who will do it for free. This is the worst possible solution. Period. It is never a good idea to ask for a favor that relates to business. NEVER. So let me try my very best to talk you out of this. I know your Cousin Bob loves you and he wants to help you out. He has built some websites before and he has offered to do yours for you for free. I know this sounds like a really good deal. But please, PLEASE think through the all-too-common scenarios that arise from such well-meaning gestures.

Common scenario #1

Cousin Bob builds you a website and it's awful. The colors are all wrong, or the design is half-baked. Or maybe the links don't work right, or the really cool video only plays on computers that are running Windows Vista. Or the fonts don't work with a different browser. Maybe he's included some terrific background music that he thinks is totally perfect for your website, but you disagree. Let's think about this.

How can you tell Cousin Bob that his design stinks? He did this for you as a favor, right? He spent hours and hours on this project. How will he feel if you totally hate the design? How will YOU feel? Will you be willing to have an awful website representing your business? Or will you be willing to insult Cousin Bob and risk alienating your favorite family member?

What about the music he chose? You ask him, "Is it legal to use that song on my website?" And he replies, "Do you really think Def Leppard is surfing the web, looking to see if your website violates their copyright?" How will you respond to that? After all the work he did for free, will you be willing to tell him it doesn't work for you and your business?

And speaking of copyrights, where did Cousin Bob get those pictures? Is he well versed in the copyright laws? If he purchased pictures for your site, has he read the licensing agreements? Are you willing to accept the liability for using images that may violate copyright and licensing laws? I promise you the judge won't care who built the site. You as the owner are responsible for its content. If Cousin Bob can't prove to you that *you* have the right to use those images, words, videos, or sounds, you need to tell him "No thanks". Please don't accept business favors from friends.

Common scenario #2

Cousin Bob creates a website, but then his life gets busy. He can't seem to find the time to get it finished. Or you have some changes you want him to make and he's too busy to get them done. Or maybe the job has gotten much bigger than he imagined when he first offered his services. Now what?

He did what he did for you at no charge, so it's really hard for you to complain. But your website is your corporate image.

It's the public face of your business plan. It's the single most important marketing tool you own. You can't accept that it isn't right, isn't working, or is outdated or incorrect.

You hate to look a gift horse in the mouth, right? But if your business depends upon the health of those teeth, you have to look. And when Cousin Bob's free web design is letting your business down, you have to complain. And that hurts when you're talking about family. Or friends. Or anyone who's doing it as a personal favor. Please don't accept business favors from friends.

Cousin Bob creates your website, and then you have a falling out. Worst-case scenario: He does something malicious to your site. Best-case scenario: He stops answering your calls.

Please don't think that this can't happen to you. It can and it does happen to business owners just like you. If Cousin Bob is really angry, he can deal your business some serious pain. He has full access to your website and can post anything he likes on there. Anything. Maybe he replaces your homepage with a notice that you've gone out of business and are now referring your clients to a competitor. OUCH! Or maybe he posts some nasty pictures on your homepage. The possibilities are limited only by the limits of Cousin Bob's vindictive imagination.

In the best-case scenario, Cousin Bob just stops answering your calls. It's not as malicious, but it still can hurt your business.

If he controls the passwords, he controls your website. And gaining control back from him can prove a frustrating and time-consuming process. Believe me, I've helped far too many clients recover from this pain, and it's not fun. Please don't accept business favors from friends.

All too often, a well-meaning friend becomes a business owner's biggest nightmare, and I don't want that to happen to you. So I will say it again: It is never a good idea to ask for a favor that relates to business. NEVER.

The bottom line:

It is far better to say "No Thanks" **before** Cousin Bob spends a hundred hours of his free time building you a website. Personal relationships are complicated and far too valuable to risk. And your website is too important to your business.

I've given you some sound, honest advice, and I hope you'll heed it. But if you insist on ignoring my good advice and decide to accept your friend's offer, there are some steps you can take to protect your interests. Always hope for the best, but plan for the worst.

1. Get it in writing. This protects you and Cousin Bob. Sketch out the basic layout and plan what will be included on each page.
2. Make sure the domain name is registered in *your* name, with *your* contact information.
3. Make sure you have all the usernames and passwords associated with the site, including the domain account and the hosting account.
4. Keep copies of the emails between you and the files you send him.
5. Shop around for a professional designer, just in case.

Option 3: You hire a professional. Unless the cost is absolutely out of reach, this is your best option, arguably your only good option. For all the reasons outlined above, the service of a professional designer is well worth the expense, assuming you find the right one. The following chapter is all about making sure that happens. But first, I want to clarify a common point of confusion.

The difference between a designer and a developer

These two terms are often confused, and some people mistakenly use the terms interchangeably. But the two are actually very different. When you are looking for someone to create your website, it's important to know the difference so that you can ask for – and find – someone who can do the job you need done.

A web designer is trained in the use of special software and a number of programming languages (HTML and JavaScript, for example) that allow him to create attractive, functional websites that present a message or a corporate image to the public. With a good web designer, you'll get a website that's appealing and easy to use, so your visitors will get the information they want, as well as the information you want them to have. Your website will present a corporate image that reflects well upon your business, your people, and your products and services.

But some businesses require more from their websites. In recent years, website owners have begun asking for websites that perform additional functions. E-commerce sites, for example require another level of expertise, as do websites that work with databases. Some websites require a login and password in order to protect sensitive information, while others provide interactive programs that give the user unique feedback, instant price quotes, or other complex calculations. The programs that run these websites are built by web developers, and there's almost no limit to what a good web developer can create.

Many web designers are able to offer some of the functionality once limited to the realm of the developer by using commercial software that provide some of the more common functionality such as shopping carts or online payment systems. These software programs were created by web developers, then packaged for sale to web designers. Thus, you may find a web designer who can build your website with the functionality you want, without the expense of a custom built program.

These pre-packaged products are limited in how much they can be customized, but they are usually much cheaper – often thousands of dollars cheaper - than a custom-built package.

So I recommend you start with a web designer. Discuss with him the plans you have for your website and the functions you'd like it to perform. If the site requires the work of a developer, he may be able to recommend a good one. Or he may take the project and sub-contract the developer's portion. If you've found a good designer, he'll steer you in the right direction.

Part II

How to Find a Good Web Designer

CHAPTER 4

The Horror Stories

I f you have a website, you probably have a horror story to tell that relates to that website. It seems that website ownership is almost synonymous with nightmare. And if you've tried dealing with the geeks, and help desks, and 800 numbers that are answered by someone from India whom you can't understand, you'll understand why I call it a real "DMV Experience".

I'm here to help you avoid all of that, by teaching you what to look for, what questions to ask, and what steps to take to assure – or at least make possible – a more pleasant, satisfying, and profitable website ownership experience. I begin by relating some of the more common horror stories, in the hopes of educating you to the possibilities so that you can avoid them.

While these stories are frightening, they are not uncommon. In fact, hardly a day goes by that I don't speak to someone who has experienced one or more of these horror stories. These nightmares happen ALL THE TIME to intelligent, successful business leaders. So don't think they can't happen to you. They can and they will, unless you are prepared. ***Forewarned is forearmed.***

Over the next several pages, I will be relating website ownership stories that are very frightening, and unfortunately, very true. The names have been changed to protect the innocent. These are terrifying tales, but if you can handle the truth, you can learn from it. So grab your popcorn and turn the page… if you dare!

JoEllen needed a web designer to build her website, joellenscoolstuff.net. She shopped around and asked for references. She finally settled on a company based in her hometown, who was highly recommended and whose price was a little lower than most.

A few weeks later, the website was almost finished, and her designer called to help her set up her hosting account. "A basic hosting account is $15.95/month," he explained, "but that only includes one email address. If you need more than that, you'll have to go with our Small Business package, but that's only $6.00 more."

She needed at least five email addresses. (One for herself and each of her three employees, plus an generic info@ joellenscoolstuff.net.) So she accepted the terms and agreed to pay the $21.95/month.

A few months later, she asked the designer to add two more email addresses (one for a new employee, and one called sales@ joellenscoolstuff.net.) and she asked that the latter be auto-forwarded to her main email account. The designer set up the accounts, but told her that the forwarding capability isn't standard on the Small Business hosting plan. That service was available for an additional $1.99/month.

So she was up to $23.94/month, but the site was great, it worked well, and her customers loved it. The big shocker came when she wanted to start accepting credit cards online. "That takes you into the realm of e-commerce," her designer explained. "And that requires a whole new level of complexity and security. Hosting for an e-commerce site starts at $69.95/month. Are you sure you want to do that?"

JoEllen thought about it and decided that she really needed to have the credit card capability. Her competitors had it, and her customers were demanding it. So she told the designer to go ahead and set it up.

JoEllen later learned that many hosting services offer all the features she needed for under $10/month, including e-commerce capability. But she was trapped in a long-term agreement with her web designer/hosting company. In order to change to a cheaper hosting service, she'd have to pay the early termination fee of almost a thousand dollars!

This sort of price gouging happens all the time. Shop around before you buy, and don't let it happen to you.

Horror Story #2 – The Unfinished Symphony

Jason hired a locally renowned graphic designer to design his website. The two of them sat down and mapped out what the pages were to look like and what content would be presented on each page. The designer estimated a cost of $1200, and Jason agreed to pay half up front.

The designer went to work as soon as Jason's check cleared, and he created a beautiful home page with real pizzazz and amazing visual appeal. He set up Jason's hosting account and launched the homepage so Jason and his business partners could review it and give their input. They loved it, and told the designer to go forward with the project using the design they'd seen.

For the next six weeks, Jason waited with excitement and anxiety while the designer worked his magic on the rest of the site. At one point he sent the designer an email asking for an update, and the designer said he was working on it. Two more weeks passed, and still no update, so Jason called him. "What's the status of our website?" Jason asked.

But the designer replied, "Well you never sent me the pictures I asked for. I am waiting on you."

Jason didn't remember being asked for pictures, so he got some clarification, and then went to work gathering the needed pictures. A couple of days later, Jason sent the pictures, and the wait began again.

Two weeks later, Jason called again for a status report. "Well, I got those pictures, but you didn't tell me which ones you wanted on which page." Again, the designer was blaming Jason for the delay. So Jason sat down and wrote another email, this time stating which picture he wanted on which page. And the waiting began again. This scenario just repeats ad nauseam, with the designer doing no work, and Jason being continually blamed for the delays.

Six months... a year... and Jason's website never gets finished. But the designer has been paid half up front. He doesn't care if he never sees the other half of Jason's payment. He has happily moved on to his next victim.

This is a very common problem. Web designers get paid half up front, then they sit down and do the fun part of the job – the creative design part. But when it comes time to actually earn the second half of the payment, they get bored (or find it's too hard) and they put that client on the back burner indefinitely. Don't let this happen to you.

Horror Story #3 -The Attack of the Giant Leeches

I love that title, don't you? The Giant Leeches – the web designers that latch onto an unsuspecting client, and suck him dry. This is what happened when Darnell hired a web designer to build his website. Darnell was the director of an art museum, and he wanted a website to promote the museum's permanent collection as well as visiting artists' exhibits. He shopped around for a designer with the portfolio that appealed to his artistic taste, and hired Casey to create the site. She did a fantastic job. The site was perfect - beautiful, functional, easy to navigate, and it was the perfect backdrop for the wonderful artwork that Darnell was showcasing.

On the homepage, Darnell wanted to showcase the current and upcoming exhibits, so that page would have to be changed every couple of weeks. The museum also published a monthly newsletter that they wanted posted on the website. So those updates would also be part of the regular maintenance of the site.

Each time there was to be a change to the homepage, Darnell would email Casey the artwork and text they wanted posted, and she would make the changes on the website. Every month, Darnell would also email Casey a copy of the latest newsletter and she would post it on the site. It worked like a charm. The site was always fresh and current, and visitor response was overwhelmingly positive.

The problem was in the billing. Each of the updates was received separately, so it was billed as a separate job. It might take Casey just a few minutes to perform an update, but her pricing policy stated that any design project would be billed at a minimum of one hour. So, on January 10th, the museum got invoiced for a homepage update – one hour at $125/hour. And on January 20th, they got the invoice for the newsletter update – another hour, another $125. You can see that in no time at all, the museum's website budget was out of control, and there was no way to stop it. They needed the regular updates, but they had never anticipated how costly they would become.

In the end, the museum threatened to take their business elsewhere, and Casey was forced to negotiate a maintenance package that would help the museum control and anticipate their expenses. But be aware that, had the museum tried to take their site elsewhere, they might have been assessed termination fees and/or set up fees on the other end that could have cost them handsomely.

The leeches are out there. Don't let them suck you dry.

Horror Story #4 - The Case of the Stolen Domain

Stanley had a small store in downtown Smallville where he sold teas from around the world. Business was good, but he knew he'd do better if he could sell his teas online to a larger market. So he contracted with a Designer Joe to build him a website. "I don't know anything about computers," Stanley admitted, "so the less I'm involved, the better it will be."

That was the WRONG thing to say! Those words are music to the ears of any unscrupulous web designer. If he knows you are clueless, he knows he can take advantage of you. Of course, once you've finished reading this book, you won't be clueless, but still – Don't show the guy all your cards before the negotiating begins.

So Stanley told Designer Joe to set it up and make it work, and Joe did just that. He purchased a domain name, a hosting plan, and a shopping cart program, and then he built the site and launched it. Stanley was thrilled. It was a nice site, the shopping cart was working great, and he was selling teas all over the country – and beyond.

But Designer Joe was becoming increasingly hard to work with. Stanley would email him about updates or additions to his website, and Joe wouldn't respond. His phone calls went straight to voicemail, and Joe wouldn't call him back. Stanley decided it was time to shop around for a new designer.

Stanley did his homework and found a good designer with a solid reputation for customer satisfaction. And that designer, Designs by Yvette, was willing to take over the maintenance of Stanley's website. "I'll need access to the hosting account and the domain account," Yvette explained. "You'll have to give me those passwords."

But Stanley didn't have the passwords – Only Designer Joe had them. So Stanley called Joe, emailed him, even faxed him, asking for the passwords to his domain and hosting accounts, but Joe failed to respond. Yvette did some looking into the domain registration and discovered that the domain name "Stanley-sells-teas-online.com" was registered to Designer Joe – not to Stanley.

"Now that is a problem," she told Stanley. If Joe owns the domain name, we can't touch it.

"But I own it!" Stanley insisted. "I paid for it. It's my company. I've built my business around that domain name. Of course I own it."

Yvette had seen this before. "Well, if you can get Joe to hand over the passwords, then yes, you might own it. But if he refuses, he can hold your domain hostage forever. Because legally, the records all say it belongs to him."

Stanley was coming to understand a very ugly truth. Designer Joe had purchased the domain name, using Joe's credit card and Joe's contact information. Stanley's name was never involved anywhere in the registration process.

"I'll sue him!" Stanley cried. "I paid him to do a job for me. He had no right to take control of my domain like that."

And to that, Yvette replied, "You could sue him, and I hope you do. But I know you won't and here's why. You can sue Joe, and maybe - MAYBE – you would win. But you have a business to run. And you can't wait around for two or three years while the courts decide who owns that domain name. You have to move on. You'll purchase a new domain name and build a new website using the new domain. You'll send out emails to notify all your customers of the change, and you'll have all your brochures and fliers reprinted with the new web address. And eventually, you'll get back to where you were before this nastiness occurred. But by then, you'll be busy fighting more current battles and won't have time to sue Joe over something that no longer matters."

Stanley was stunned, but he knew Yvette was right.

"I've seen this too many times to count," she said. "Designers will put everything in their own name because it's easier that way. And because they know as long as they own the domain, only they can work on the website. It's job security for them. It's unethical and it might even be illegal. But they also know the sad truth that small business owners don't have the time or money to fight that battle in the courts. "

Actually, some designers will put everything in their own name *because the customer asks them to*. If that seems strange to you, think back to when Stanley told Joe, "I don't know anything about computers, so the less I'm involved, the better it will be." Clients often hand over the keys because it's easier for them to do so. They don't want to be involved in the details. But this is one situation, where you can't afford to delegate your authority. Hold onto all the usernames and passwords. And before you begin, make sure you get it in writing that the domain, the domain name, and hosting accounts all belong to you.

Horror Story #5 - The Secret Lives of Angels

Clara ran a Christian preschool in Smallville called Little Angels Academy. She hired Rufus to build her a basic website. It was an especially awful design, but Rufus was cheap, so Clara didn't complain. At least she had a place where she could post her school calendar, lunch menus and other information the parents of her students wanted to know.

Rufus designed the homepage with a wide blue arch that stretched above the plain white center of the page. And on that arch, he placed pictures of sweet little angles with fluffy white wings. They looked like pictures cut from a magazine by a preschooler. The idea was cute, but not very well executed. Another problem I noticed was that the "Welcome" heading was partly obstructed by the blue arch. It really looked like… well, it didn't look very good.

Being a web designer, and always checking out the competition, I scrolled to the bottom of the page to see if the genius responsible for this mess was taking credit for it. Lo and behold, there it was: "Site designed by Rufus Web Design Inc." As I usually do when I encounter a new competitor, I clicked on his link to visit his website.

The link opened his website, but not in a new window which is what I expected. Instead, it opened the designer's website inside the Little Angels' website. The blue arch was still on the screen, and the fluffy-winged cherubs were floating in their assigned spots. The browser's address bar still said www.little-angels-of-smallville.com, and the school's logo was still centered at the top. But the white space in the center of the page was filled up with the Rufus Web Design homepage.

Now I must admit it's a flaw in my character that leads me to seek out the shortcomings in my competitors. I take way too much pleasure in finding fault with their work and knowing that I'd have done it better. I'm sure I'll suffer in the afterlife for this flaw, but the boost it gives my ego is powerful motivation in the here and now. So when I saw this really awful example of web design, I was appalled by the shoddy workmanship, but I wanted to see more. So I clicked on the button marked "My Portfolio".

Rufus's portfolio page opened up, still in the same window with the Little Angels floating overhead. And on that page were links to all the sites Rufus had designed. One of those links said "Gallery ABC – Smallville's premier art studio". Well, I knew that a new art studio had just opened in downtown Smallville, and I was (being something of an artist myself) interested in seeing their website. So I clicked… Oh dear.

There I was, staring at the homepage of Gallery ABC, but it was no art gallery's site. Gallery ABC was a portal to a porn site! The photo of a nearly naked woman in an erotic pose was staring back at me, coaxing me to click on links that would undoubtedly lead me down the seedier back streets of the Internet. There I was, looking at a pornographic gateway, while the fluffy little angels floated over the scene. I was still on the Little Angels' website. My browser's address bar still said www.little-angels-of-smallville.com, and the school's logo was still centered at the top. But in the center of the page, where Clara had planned to display the school lunch menu, I was viewing a very different fare. I'm pretty sure that's not what Clara had in mind when she hired Rufus to build her website.

This story is absolutely true. The names of the preschool, the town, the gallery, and the web designer have been changed. And in real-life, it wasn't a preschool, but a community organization that was the unsuspecting victim. I don't honestly believe "Rufus" had any malicious intent toward his client. I believe he just didn't know what he was doing. In the early days of web design, this "style" of website was relatively common practice. And let's face it. If I had chosen a different link from his portfolio, the story wouldn't have been nearly so dramatic. But the truth is, I did choose that link, and it did open a porn portal, and it did so under the Little Angel's banner and logo. So whether Rufus was inept, or lazy, or strangely demented, the result was a huge embarrassment, and potentially much worse.

While this story is a dramatic example, it illustrates a vitally important point. Your web designer holds the keys to your public image. And the content of your website is out there for all the world to see. If your designer is lazy, or uninformed, or careless, or devious, you could wind up with content on your website that you didn't intend.

Never forget that the content of your website is your responsibility, and no one else's. Even if you hire a great designer with an outstanding work ethic, remarkable skill, and unquestionable integrity, you owe it to yourself to check his work. Test the links, proofread the text, and remember that it's your public image out there.

Horror Story #6 - Now you see me – Now you don't

Phil was a highly skilled chef with years of experience in the restaurant business, and had finally saved enough money to open his own restaurant. A few days after registering his business, he got a call from "Dan Dan the Website Man". Phil knew he needed a website and knew he needed a professional to create it, so when Dan called, Phil was open to discussing his website needs. He told Dan, "I just want a basic site – nothing too flashy, just a place to put my hours and my menu." But Dan had other suggestions. "Maybe you'd like to post special events? Maybe coupons your visitors can download? How about a newsletter?"

Dan explained that these were good things to include in a website because they would help draw visitors to the site and encourage those visitors to visit Phil's restaurant. And Dan agreed that he could use those things as well. Then Dan talked to him about Search Engine Optimization. "That's really necessary if you want people to find you on Google," Dan told him. And Phil agreed.

"Now I want you to consider a website analysis package. This feature allows you to determine who is visiting your site, which pages they are visiting, how long they are staying, and how they found your site. This is very important information so that you can know how well your site is really working for you and what pages are the most effective and which ones are the least effective."

The conversation continued and Phil found that the "basic site" he had envisioned was turning into a lot of money. When Dan gave him the grand total, Phil almost fainted. But Dan said he could set up a payment plan to make it manageable. "You'll pay me half up front, but then the remainder can be paid off in monthly payments with 0% interest." It was a big investment, much more than he had expected to spend, but with the payment plan, it seemed feasible to Phil.

They talked about color schemes and design concepts and Phil was getting excited about the beautiful website he and Dan would be building together. He mailed a check for the down payment, and the two of them went to work, building the website.

Phil spent much of the next week gathering content and perfecting the wording he wanted on each page of his site. Every day or two, he would email new content to Dan, and Dan would reply that he had received it and would be incorporating the new content into Phil's website. Phil couldn't wait to see the whole project live on the Internet.

But the website was never built. Once the check had cleared, Dan stopped replying to Phil's emails and voicemails, and every attempt Phil made to get in touch with Dan failed. Even the address where he had mailed the check proved to be a dead end. Phil had invested hundreds in the down payment, but his designer was nowhere to be found. Dan had cashed his check and disappeared.

Phil had to decide if it was worth his time and effort to try to track Dan down and get his money back. How much time would that take? Between the police reports, interviews, and endless forms, Phil knew he'd spend many hours trying to recover his money. But he was trying to open a new restaurant and had precious little time to spare. "Besides," he thought, "how much money could I honestly expect to recover if I ever did find him?" In the end, Phil just accepted that he'd made a lousy business decision and hoped his budget would survive the hit. He had learned a good lesson, but it had cost him plenty.

The Moral of the Story

Now that I've told you some of the more common horror stories, you might be thinking it would be wiser to just build your site yourself. But that is almost never the best option. Although the opportunity to get ripped off is definitely present, your ability to protect yourself is much greater because you have been forewarned. And the rest of this book will be full of good advice and sound strategies that will help you avoid these and other horror stories with your own designer.

In the Horror Story #1, "The Host of a Different Color", you learned that hosting charges vary greatly from one provider to the next, and that some providers are more than happy to charge you for features you don't need, while others charge you extra for features you can get in a basic (and inexpensive) package elsewhere. In Chapter 8 I'll be talking more about hosting providers and how you can find one that meets your needs at a fair and honest price.

In the Horror Story #2, "The Unfinished Symphony", you learned that some designers are more interested in the initial creative process than in actually completing the job. Later in this chapter, I'll tell you how to identify the designers who will complete your project on time and with professional results.

Horror Story #3, "The Attack of the Giant Leeches", demonstrated that some designers will undercharge for the initial design, but then lock you into paying exorbitant prices for regular updates and maintenance. In Chapter 7, we'll talk more about maintenance fees and maintenance agreements. You'll learn how to estimate your time requirements and how to find a designer that offers the maintenance package that will work for you.

In the Horror Story #4, "The Case of the Stolen Domain", I warned you about designers that keep tight control over their clients' domains – even putting them in their own names – so that only they can work on the websites. A designer that holds a domain hostage guarantees that you won't take your business elsewhere, so he's under no pressure to provide good service. Later, I'll explain how to prevent this scenario from taking over your website.

Horror Story #5, "The Secret Lives of Angels", is a vivid example of what can happen when you turn over the keys to an unskilled or unscrupulous designer. This chapter, and others throughout this book, are dedicated to helping you find a good designer and prevent the nightmares associated with inept or corrupt "professionals".

And finally, we talked about outright fraud in Horror Story #6, "Now You See Me – Now You Don't". While web designers don't have the corner on this market, I believe that the opportunity for con men and women to steal from business people like you is perhaps more prevalent than in other industries. Owners of small business know they need a website, but they don't know much about the processes involved. So an unethical designer can talk the talk, and lead the willing and uninformed down a rosy path that leads nowhere. This is an unregulated industry, meaning that there are no government watchdogs looking out for the consumer's interests. So the need to be an informed consumer is greater than in many other industries.

Fortunately, you are doing your homework. This book was written to teach you several tips and strategies that will empower you to understand the lingo, ask the right questions, and avoid handing your money over to the wrong kinds of people. By reading this book, and following the advice presented here, you are improving your odds enormously. Avoid the horror stories - Read on!

CHAPTER 5

Geeks and Artistes

Most website designers fall into one of two categories. They are either Geeks or they are Artistes. The purpose of this section is to help you understand the minds of these two types of designers so that you can make an informed decision when it comes to choosing a web designer. So first, let me define these labels I've chosen to use to describe the two categories of designers.

For the purpose of this book, I define a geek as a person who is highly skilled in computer technology, and often obsessed with technical pursuits. While this was once a derogatory term, many modern geeks have come to accept – and even embrace – the term. They wear it like a badge of honor.

The true geek is a left-brain thinker. Logical, analytical, and precise. These are the attributes that make for a good systems administrator. The best geeks will assure that the websites they build are technically sound and functional. The links will work, the database interactions will be flawless, and the layout will be based upon a logical progression of data flow. You definitely want a good geek to handle your hosting needs because that is a purely technical endeavor, and that is where the geek's talents really shine.

Geeks go by many names, including Network Technicians, Computer (or IT) Specialists, Computer (or IT) Engineers, and other variations on the Computer, Network, or IT themes.

An artiste, on the other hand, is a purely right-brain thinker. He is an artist, often an entertainer, and always in pursuit of challenges to – and outlets for - his own creativity. The artiste has a strong sense of color and visual appeal, and is capable of thinking outside the box. Creativity is his strength and his motivator, and he is driven by the desire to wow the audience.

So now that I have defined the two stereotypes, I want to focus on how to use your knowledge of these personality types when you are looking for the right web designer for your own business.

Geeks make the worst web designers.

It is my contention that geeks make the absolutely worst web designers, and I'm about to tell you why. But first, let me insert my disclaimer that of course, there are always exceptions to every rule. And there probably are true geeks out there who are great designers. Let me also state for the record that I myself am trained as a geek. I have a bachelor's degree in Information Systems Management, am a Certified Network Technician, and long-time computer tech for various entities in the public and private sectors. I have worked in the geek departments, alongside a number of true geeks; I've even served in Iraq with the geeks of the US Army. I've never shared their passion for the technical puzzle, but I think that I can say, with at least a modicum of authority, that I know something about geeks. And the first thing I know about them is that quite often, their technical skills are stronger than their people skills. I know this is a cliché, but it got to be a cliché because it is true. To put it rather bluntly, geeks aren't that good with people - It's why they are so good with computers.

While that may be a gross generalization, and I may have exaggerated the point for the sake of illustration, I do think it is essentially true, and few geeks I've spoken to have disputed the general premise, which simply stated is, "Geeks don't do people. That's why they are good at computers."

When a geek sits down to design a website, his first interest in the project is the technical puzzle. You, as a business owner, don't care two figs about the technical puzzle, but that is the true geeks highest motivation. The very *last* thing the true geek cares about is the audience. Yet, I would argue that the audience is the single most important consideration for a web designer.

Good web design requires a very different skill set. It requires empathy with the audience, because the main purpose of a website is to communicate with people. But if geeks were good at communicating with people, they wouldn't be geeks!

When I sit down to a new website project, the first question I ask myself is, "Who is my audience and how can I best communicate this message to that audience?" I need to put myself in their shoes, look at the website from their perspective, and build it from the ground up with that perspective in mind. My experience with geeks has taught me that the audience is usually the very last thing to enter the mind of a true geek. This is why I believe that geeks make the absolutely worst web designers.

Why, then, is it true that most websites are actually designed by geeks? Part of the answer to that question lies in the history of the Internet. Historically, the Internet has been the realm of geeks. They were the ones who first understood its potential, and they were the ones with the programming skills to create those early websites. And real web design does involve using those programming skills, although modern software has lessened the degree to which a designer must rely upon those skills.

Geeks continue to be the web designers of choice for another reason – They market themselves as web designers. Their clients and potential clients expect them to be web designers. The general public has very little knowledge of how websites are created; they only know "it's computer stuff". So they look to the computer experts and assume they'll have the skills to do the job.

But I believe this is akin to asking a taxidermist to perform surgery on a live animal. Sure, he has all the tools, and a knowledge of anatomy. But the skills he's missing are *really* important. It's the same in web design.

A geek may have the tools and the skills to use those tools. But the purpose of a website is to communicate with people, and that is usually not one of the true geek's greatest strengths.

You may find that, within your geographic location (or your budget) the only web designers you can find are geeks. That's OK, because in later in this chapter, I'm going to teach you what to look for, and what questions to ask, so that you find the very best designer for your specific needs, whether he's a geek or an artiste.

Artistes make the second worst web designers.

So let's have a look at those artistes, because if your designer isn't a geek, he's probably an artiste. Sometimes they call themselves Digital Artists, Commercial Artist, or Graphic Designers, and they can be very different creatures from the bashful geeks we've been discussing.

An artiste is motivated by the creative process. He approaches each web design project with enthusiasm and vigor and can't wait to set some paint on the digital canvas. His realm is the world of color and hue, of shape and line, of balance and symmetry. A true artiste will design a web site that is eye-catching, attractive, visually appealing, and expressive – according to his own sense of those things.

The artiste's design will definitely make a statement, and you definitely want your website to make a statement. But hopefully it will be the statement you have in mind for your audience. Because if it's not, you may discover why the stereotype describes artistes as "temperamental".

The first reason I don't recommend true artistes as web designers is that they can, indeed, be very temperamental. Their designs are truly extensions of themselves, and they pour their souls into the creative process. If you don't like the result, they may be deeply insulted, or they may dismiss your opinion as uninformed. Either way, disagreements like this can make it difficult for the two of you to find common ground and work together to create the website you want and need.

A far more serious reason for avoiding the pure artiste is his lack of interest in the non-creative work. I can't tell you how many times I've heard the complaint. "Pierre" designs a site and it's beautiful! The colors, the flair, the wild creativity! But then he loses interest. When it is time to spend the long hours just tweaking content or verifying that the links are working, he just can't manage to get it done. The project gets put on Pierre's back burner while he goes out and grabs the next creative challenge. He gets bored with the mundane work and all the minute details, so he just moves on. It happens all the time. Pierre stops answering his phone, or maybe he'll do a little bit to appease a frantic client, and then he'll slide away again, looking for his next creative fix. The whole project leaves the business owner in the lurch, frustrated and out of options. The designer in Horror Story #2, The Unfinished Symphony, was almost certainly an artiste.

The third reason I am leery of artistes in the web design world is that they tend to focus more on their own creative production, rather than the audience's experience. In essence, the artiste looks at a website as his canvas, and can almost forget that it's not his own message that matters. You, the business owner, have paid him to present *your* message, but sometimes that message can get lost. All too often, the true artiste creates an image of his own vision, seeking a reaction from the audience to his own talent. They are performers, yearning for applause. Artistes sometimes forget that the whole project isn't all about them.

So where does that leave you?

I've told you that almost all web designers are either geeks or artistes. And I've told you that neither of these groups make especially good web designers. So what's left for you to do? Fear not! The rest of this chapter – and indeed the whole book – will help you find someone who is "just right". Or at the very least, it will help you work with the geek or artiste you choose to get the best possible results.

The designer you want will have enough technical skill and enough artistic vision to fulfill the job's requirements. But above all, the designer you want will be what I call an "**artful communicator**". He'll be great at the art of communication. He'll be able to talk to you in plain, simple English, and will be willing to take the time to explain any technical details you need to understand.

The designer you want will be able to communicate with your audience. After all, that is the primary purpose of a website. He will be able to use technology and art as tools to artfully communicate *your message* so that *your audience* hears it loud and clear. He'll capture their attention and hold it, because that's what needs to happen in order to communicate your message. He'll portray your business in the manner that suits your message. He'll understand your audience, and will design a website that speaks to them. And he'll do it artfully, incorporating the visual impact that will support the message you want your audience to hear.

> Your website is your corporate image. Your web designer needs to understand that and be able to communicate that image to the audience you are trying to reach. The **artful communicator** understands people. He's motivated by the challenges of communicating to people. He recognizes the demographic differences that make up the target audience, and he's excited by the challenge of capturing and captivating that audience.

The rest of this book will help you find such a designer, or at least improve your odds. And the knowledge you'll gain from this book will help you – and your designer – improve the quality of your website. So read on!

CHAPTER 6

Integrity is Everything

This section on integrity is not a long one, but it is perhaps the most important section of the entire book. Indeed, if you take away only one lesson from having read this book, I hope it will be this:

> The less you know about website design and hosting, the more you really need a designer you can trust.

If you read through the Horror Stories in Chapter 4, you'll understand that the opportunity to get ripped off is ubiquitous. Unless you live in a cave, you already know that unscrupulous "professionals" exist in every industry. I believe that the web design industry may be even more prone to dishonesty and corruption than most other industries, simply because the factors exist that make it possible. Consider the following factors that serve to exacerbate the problem.

- **Every business needs a website**, and every website needs to be updated periodically. Most people don't have the technical skills necessary to build a website from scratch. Nor do they have the skills, time, patience, and knowledge to make any but the most minor edits to the typical website template. And the software that allows the professional web designer to work efficiently and creatively is expensive to purchase and difficult to master. Every business owner who has neither the time, the expertise, nor the inclination to do it himself must to hire a designer to build and maintain their websites.

- **Good help is hard to find.** This adage is especially true in the world of web design. Lots of designers have the knowledge and the resources required to create and maintain a website is limited. But the number of those who can create a truly effective website is actually quite small. And **artful communicators** with both technical skill and artistic vision are rare indeed.

- **Knowledge is power.** The people who do have the knowledge and skills to address the growing needs of the Internet are in a powerful position. It's like when I take my car to a mechanic. I know nothing about cars, and that mechanic knows it. From the moment I roll my car onto his parking lot, I'm at his mercy. If he tells me I need a new whatsit, who am I to argue? If he tells me he has to completely disassemble my car to replace the existing whatsit, how can I question his opinion? And if he tells me the procedure is critical to the safe operation of my vehicle, I'll be writing the check. It won't matter if that whatsit costs $50 or $500. I'll be writing that check. I might suspect he's lying to me. I might even take it for a second opinion. But most of the time, I'm just going to write the check and curse my own ignorance. It's the same with web designers. They have the knowledge and their customers don't. And that gives them enormous power.

  When an uninformed business owner calls a web designer to inquire about a new website, the business owner is immediately at the designer's mercy. He knows he needs a website, but he has absolutely no idea how much it should cost. He doesn't know if it will be three hundred dollars, or three thousand, or thirty thousand. He just knows he needs one. And the designer at the other end of the line *knows* he doesn't know.

All too often, the business owner makes matters worse by announcing at the start that, "I know nothing about this stuff." Big mistake, folks. Very big mistake.

- **Power corrupts.** It's been true since long before Lord Acton penned the famous line about absolute power corrupting absolutely. Web designers are empowered by the knowledge they hold over their clients and by their clients' need for their services. With all that power comes the temptation to exploit for personal gain. The temptation is there to stretch the truth, inflate the costs, or overstate the challenges. Your designer might tell you that a feature you hope to add to your website requires a higher level of security, or a greater commitment of his time, or a higher level of development expertise. And any or all of that might be true. Or it might not be true. The point is, you won't know. You can't be expected to know such details unless you have experience in the web design world. You'll necessarily be at his mercy, and he knows it. You are going to have to *trust* him. But remember these words on the subject from Abraham Lincoln. "If you want to test a man's character, give him power."

- **Integrity is learned.** Call it integrity, or call it ethics. Call it honesty, or just knowing right from wrong. Whatever you call it, we Americans have traditionally learned it from our parents. I know I got my integrity from my mother. Her honesty, her work ethic, and her sense of right and wrong were apparent to me from my earliest recollection. It wasn't necessarily her religion that led her down the paths she walked, but her innate sense of what was right. She was a person you could trust. And I like to think my own integrity is a reflection of hers. I strive for it to be.

But for too many people in our society, the lines between right and wrong, between what is fair and what is simply acceptable, have been blurred. We no longer coach our kids to "play fair"; we coach them to "play to win". And all too often, we come to accept that an action, however dishonest or unjust, is acceptable as long as you don't get caught.

I believe that many Americans, especially the younger ones who have never had to truly sacrifice, have not yet developed a real work ethic. And I contend that the web design industry has more than its share of these untested, and unhardened young people. They get out of school, get themselves some bootleg software, and proclaim themselves to be "IT Professionals". With the title, comes the expectation of earning a comfortable income, while sleeping till noon, knocking off at three, and playing golf all weekend. For many, the idea of starting at the bottom and working your way up the ladder has been completely replaced by the notion that a college degree entitles you to start at the top and relax there.

Without a genuine work ethic, and often without an ethic of any kind, these people prey upon the uninformed to provide them the ridiculous incomes they think they deserve, but are unwilling to work for. They run their con on unsuspecting business owners, and when the going gets tough, they just retreat.

Fortunately, there are web designers out there who do have integrity and a solid work ethic. You just have to do your homework to make sure the one you hire is one of the good guys.

CHAPTER 7

Maintaining Your Website

Once you have your website up and running, it needs to be updated – often! For one thing, Google likes websites that are frequently updated. But more importantly, you customers and potential customers expect it. When a visitor looks at a website that hasn't been changed in over a year, that tells them that the business owners aren't all that interested in communicating with online visitors. Or worse, it might tell them that the business owners don't have their corporate act together. It might even imply to your visitor that your business has gone out of business.

Repeat visitors – your regular customers – want to see fresh and interesting changes the next time they come back. And if they see the same-old-same-old, they'll lose interest. I really want you to understand that the content and condition of your website speaks volumes about your business. It really is you corporate image. So please don't let it get stale and moldy just sitting on the shelf. Your website needs continual attention, also known as website maintenance.

Who creates the updates and how they will be implemented is a discussion for you and your designer. But I strongly encourage you to work out a maintenance plan with your designer, for all the same reasons I advised you to hire him in the first place.

The good news is that once you have your website built, you can usually have it maintained at a very reasonable rate. Most designers offer maintenance plans that provide for regular updates for less than the designer's usual hourly rate, and sometimes these plans include priority service, meaning that your updates would be bumped to the front of the line when the designer's calendar is especially full. Priority service alone is a powerful incentive to sign on for a maintenance plan, because when you see a need for a change to your site, you don't want to fall to the back of the line for service.

Pricing plans vary widely, and are almost always negotiable. So if one designer offers a plan for maintenance that appeals to you, it might be available to you from another designer, but only if you ask. Some designers have a hard and set hourly rate and they won't budge from it. Others offer a discounted rate if you are willing to sign up for a full year of service or are willing to pre-pay.

Be certain you understand going in exactly what services are covered by your maintenance plan and which ones aren't. Typically, simple updates and changes to text and pictures will be included. Uploading your monthly newsletter might be included as well. But if you wanted to add a new page (which would require a rework of the navigation and site map), such a change would likely not be included. Other designers offer a discounted hourly rate to their maintenance clients and will do whatever projects you need done for that discounted rate. Of course, you have to be sure you're dealing with a trustworthy designer who won't simply pad their hours and then discount the rate.

The bottom line is that you need to negotiate a deal for maintenance that will serve your needs without breaking your budget. If you're happy with the designer who built your site, he's the logical (and probably least expensive) choice for maintaining it. Be aware that it's far easier to work on an existing site that you built yourself than it is to work on someone else's code. So if you are hiring someone else to maintain it, the hours he'll spend on it could be substantially greater, depending on the complexity of the site and of your updates.

CHAPTER 8

One-Stop Shops: Pros and Cons

Many of the web designers in your area are probably IT networking professionals who also do web design. There are certainly advantages to getting all your IT services in one place, but there are some disadvantages too. So I think a discussion of the pros and cons of this arrangement is in order. We'll start with the advantages.

First let's consider what we actually mean by "IT services" because not every IT service company offers the same services. Here's a list of services that you may eventually need that could be offered by the IT professionals in your area.

- Network setup and configuration. These folks come to your office and set up your local network, hook up your internet connections, and configure your computers so they can share files and printers.

- Computer repair. If your computer crashes or gets a virus, these guys can fix it. Some services will come to your office to do repairs, while others ask that you bring the offending machines to them.

- Email hosting. If you have multiple people in your organization and they are all using Microsoft Outlook for their email, you might well want the services of an Exchange Server. That will enable calendar sharing and a number of other networking features that are very popular in American businesses today. These IT pros would maintain the Exchange Server, manage user accounts, reset passwords, and the like.

- Database design and management. If you need a database to track your various business entities, whether it's online or on a computer in your office, you'll need someone with database expertise to design and maintain it.

- Website hosting. These are the guys that maintain the servers that host your website and post it to the Internet.

- Website design. These are the guys who create the layout, design the visuals, and format your website into something you and your customers can use on the Internet. If you've read the previous chapters, you already have a good idea what they can do for you.

- Search Engine Optimization. If your business is dependent upon Internet traffic to bring you a substantial percentage of your business, you will need a SEO expert. These guys work with your website's content, structure, and other elements to improve your placement on search engine results pages.

There are certainly other IT services that any given IT shop might offer, but these are the most common ones. So let's consider the advantages to having all those services under one roof.

1. One company, one bill. It makes your bookkeeping and bill paying simpler if you have only one company to deal with.

2. One contact person. This can be a huge advantage – if it's available. With a single go-to guy, you can develop a relationship and get personal attention. Because the company will be meeting multiple needs, you'll have more opportunities to develop that relationship. Building that relationship could mean bumping your job ahead in the queue when you really need it.

3. When something goes wrong, there's never any question about who to call.

4. When something goes wrong, there will be less finger pointing. Some IT techs have been known to "blame the other guy" for all the IT problems. If the other guy is in the same company, there should be less of that.

5. Bulk pricing. If you are signing up for a wide range of services from the same company, you should be able to negotiate a better price than if you're just coming to them for one service.

Those are all powerful reasons to consider the one-stop-shop for all your IT needs. But let's now consider the flip side of the argument. Here are some advantages to purchasing your IT services from separate companies.

1. One contact person – at each service provider. You are probably more likely to get personal attention from a smaller single-service provider than from a large one-stop-shop. As you shop around, you'll get a sense of which companies are more personal and which ones are just too big for your comfort levels.

2. Low overhead pricing. Bigger businesses often have bigger overheads, so their pricing might actually be higher than a single-service provider. Again, as you shop around, you'll get a feel for where the best deals are.

3. Smaller failure point. This could turn out to be a very big deal for your business. If you have all your IT eggs in one basket, and that basket goes belly up, or fails to provide adequate service, you will feel some serious pain while you work to replace them. But if you have your IT services

spread out over multiple companies, and one of them fails, the rest of your services will continue to run while you work to replace the one that's failed. And often, the remaining provider can actually help you through the transition.

4. Specialized expertise. You already know that I think that geeks make the worst web designers. So it follows that I think you should hire a designer to do your design work and a geek to do your IT work. And if you need a database geek, don't ask a network tech to do that either. The skill packet required for each of these fields is different from each of the others. And I don't believe any one person can be really great at all of them.

   You wouldn't hire a radiologist to remove your kid's tonsils, now would you? Sure, they both graduated from medical school, but they have specialists for a reason, and it's the same with IT. No one can know everything, especially in a field that changes as quickly as the computer field. So in order for you to get the very best service and take advantage of the latest technologies, you really have to go to the specialists.

   Of course, you may find a single company that has several specialists on staff. That might be the best possible solution, if it's true. But beware of the geek in designer's clothing and don't get stuck in a relationship with someone who thinks he's the perfect person for every job. He's not.

I've already spoken at length about how to choose the best web designer for your business, so now I want to give you some pointers about choosing a hosting service.

First of all, your designer probably has a hosting service that he is happy to recommend. There are a number of reasons for a designer to recommend a hosting service, and you should understand these reasons before you blindly accept his recommendation.

1. If your designer is recommending a single hosting company (as opposed to offering you options), he's probably getting a kickback from the company. Call it a finder's fee or referral bonus – his own financial stake may be a big reason for his recommendation.

   That's not to say the hosting service isn't actually the best solution your designer knows. In fact, it might very well be. The truth is that most hosting services offer referral programs that pay cash for new clients. And your designer may have shopped around and decided on the very best service with which to associate himself. So just because the designer's getting a cut doesn't mean the service isn't first rate. It just means he's getting a cut.

2. Another reason designers sometimes recommend one hosting service over another is his own familiarity and

personal comfort level with that provider. If your designer has used a provider in the past and has been happy with the service and support he's received, it makes sense that he'd prefer to work with that provider again. Every hosting service has their own unique procedures and user interfaces, and some are easier for your designer to work with than others. You can be sure that he's had a positive experience with any provider he recommends. In this case, his recommendation carries some weight, especially if you will have to work directly with the provider in the future. Knowing that your designer approves of the support they provide tells you something, and it could prove valuable in the future.

3. If your website includes a shopping cart or other database functionality, your designer may recommend a specific hosting service because of their reputation for service to those specific needs.

Whatever his motivation for recommending a hosting service, your designer should be willing to entertain other options if you wish. So you should take his recommendation and check it out. Visit their website and a number of others. Compare prices and features, and speak to their sales team on the phone. You can learn a lot about a company's support system from how well their sales staff handles inquiries.

A weak sales team may indicate that the after-sale service may also be unsatisfactory.

Here are some basic features you need to compare:

- **Number of email accounts.** Some plans give you only one, and charge you extra for additional addresses. You'll need one for every employee of the business plus some extras like info@ and sales@. Look for a hosting plan that offers plenty of email accounts.
- **Storage space.** This is especially critical if you're hosting a shopping cart or other database files. If you outgrow your storage space, you'll have to upgrade your plan and that will cost you more than buying the right plan to begin with.
- **Bandwidth.** This is the amount of data that flows between your website and your visitors each month. If you expect thousands of visitors and they are all downloading big files, that would mean you'd be using a ton of bandwidth. Again, be sure you have plenty because it's usually cheaper to start with a plan that includes lots of bandwidth than it would be to start with a smaller plan and upgrade later.
- **FTP accounts.** If you have multiple employees who will be updating your website, each one should have their own FTP account. If you don't know what that is, ask the sales rep. I'll include a definition in the

glossary, but that's the kind of question that can help you assess the usefulness and the knowledge of the sales team.

- **Email forwarding.** Some hosting providers charge extra for the ability to forward email, while others include it for free. Many website owners like to have a generic email address like info@mycompany.com as well as other special accounts, and have them all forwarded to the owner's inbox or forwarded to the appropriate staff member's inbox). That allows you to post contact addresses on your website without posting your personal email address for the whole world to see.

- **Support services.** Lots of hosting providers will tell you they have 24/7 support, but what they don't tell you about their support can be a real problem when you need help. That 24/7 support – Is it a live human on the phone? Or is it only via email and online forums? When your email stops working the night before a big sales pitch, and you can't get your partner's charts for the presentation, you really want a live person to talk to. And if they have live humans, are they Americans? Now don't sick the political correctness police on me. I know that the support I get from staffers in India is first-rate support, but I personally find it difficult to communicate with them. I'll gladly pay extra for a support tech who speaks my brand of American English.

There are many other features that you may need to compare, depending upon the scope, complexity, and purpose of your website. As you shop around on a number of hosting websites, you'll start to recognize the features that most appeal to you. Take your time and take careful notes. And once you've decided on a hosting service, run it past your designer before you sign up. Make sure he has no technical objections to the service you've chosen and ask his advice. His experience may well save you a mountain of headaches over the lifetime of your website.

So whom do I recommend?

You would probably appreciate it if I'd just tell you the name of my favorite hosting provider. But there are way too many factors to consider for me to make a single blanket recommendation. I've had good luck with several hosting providers and lousy luck with others.

I will go out on a limb and say that America's leading provider, GoDaddy, is among my least favorites. Their support staff is pretty good and their pricing isn't bad. But I find their website and their entire user interface to be complicated and difficult to get around. I've had plenty of clients that just love them, though, so I'm willing to concede that there's room for personal preference.

I will tell you a great place to start is a website called RateMyHost.com. They do independent reviews of lots of hosting companies and rate their favorites. I've noticed that they aren't always up-to-date on the features and pricing of the providers they rate, but it will give you a place to start so you know a few providers worth checking out.

CHAPTER 9

Doing Your Homework

In this chapter, you're going to learn how to locate the best web designers and how to choose one that will work well for you and your business. Unfortunately, there's no directory on the web – or anywhere else – that lists all the talented, diligent, honest, web designers. So you're going to have to do some homework. The good news is that the time you invest in this will be worth your while, not only in finding a good designer, but in many other areas of your business as well.

Step 1: Designer or Developer?

The first step in choosing the right designer is to determine whether you need a web designer or a web developer. This is critical because if you choose the wrong one, you could be throwing away a lot of money. If you don't know the difference between the two, go back to Chapter 3, where I explain which is which.

Next, you'll need to look around for potential designers. A good place to start might be your local Chamber of Commerce. They will happily give you the names of all the web designers who are current members of the Chamber. Please understand, however, that the Chamber of Commerce is not in the business of *recommending* companies. They have an equal responsibility to each of their member companies, so they can *refer* you to a company because that company is one of its members. But they can't *recommend* one company over another.

And being a member of a Chamber of Commerce usually means simply that the company has paid its annual membership dues. You can't assume, just because the company has joined the local Chamber, that it is any more or less ethical, competent, or trustworthy than a company who hasn't joined the Chamber. You can only assume that they have decided that Chamber membership fits within their marketing strategy and their marketing budget.

Another way to locate web designers is to look for them on the Internet. On the Internet, you can locate companies all over the globe that can create websites that meet your needs. You don't necessarily have to choose a local company, although there are some obvious advantages to working with someone local.

Once you have a list of potential designers, check them out on the web. Have a close and critical look at each designer's own website. Is it a good site? Is it easy to get around? Is it attractive and professional looking? And most importantly, does it communicate artfully?

By looking critically at the designer's website, you should be able to tell a great deal about his ability to communicate to an audience. As you look through the pages of his website, ask yourself these questions. They will help you determine if he's a geek or an artiste, or if maybe he's the artful communicator you're really looking for.

- Is his site cluttered or confusing? If so, he's missed the mark. A website is only powerful if it's easy for the visitor to use. If it's cluttered or confusing, it won't sell anything. Website visitors have a very short attention span. They want quick, easy answers to their questions, and a confusing web page won't hold their interest. They'll dump you and move on to the next website. If your web designer's own site is a mess, you can be assured that he just doesn't get it.

- Are his grammar and spelling perfect? If not, that should tell you something about his attention to detail. If he's too lazy to spell check his own website, how careful will he be with yours? Maybe spelling isn't your strong suit either, and maybe you don't care that much about proper grammar. Let me warn you that there are plenty of people out there – people who might be your potential customers – for whom grammar is an indication of work ethic. For many people, shoddy grammar and spelling are tell tale signs of shoddy workmanship. A website that's riddled with errors tells visitors that this is a company that doesn't have its corporate act together. If the designer doesn't care to put his own house in order, can you honestly expect him to do a better job on yours?

- Is his site more concerned with his artistic expression than it is with artful communication? If so, he's definitely not your man. If his site is really cool to look at, but not so easy to navigate, maybe he's more of an artiste than a communicator. Remember that artistes are more interested in their own artistic expression than in expressing your message to your audience. Artistic vision is a wonderful tool for communicating your message, but it cannot be the message. Beware the designer whose art has become the message.

- Is his site ugly? You might be surprised at how many web designers really suck at design. These will be the true geek sites. Every website, regardless of its audience or its owner, should be a clean, attractive, and professional vision of the company's corporate image. A web designer whose own site isn't clean, attractive and professional looking, is not an artful communicator.

Whether the image you're looking for is purely professional, or whether you are hoping for a casual, or fun-and-fantasy image, your website should reflect that image. But casual doesn't mean sloppy, and fun doesn't mean haphazard. The site should have a unified look and feel throughout all the pages. Headings should match from one page to the next, and colors should compliment the design, and make the text easier to read. Although the purpose of colored text should be to enhance the readability and draw attention to specific words, all to often, designers use colors that actually make the text harder to read.

Before you agree to pay a designer, make sure he knows something about design, because that first impression is a lasting one. If his own website doesn't capture your interest, and impress you, you'll be fighting a losing battle.

- Is his site working? It's always a shock to me when I find web designers whose own sites are non-functional. I find it unforgivable that a designer would post the words "Under Construction" on their own website. If the Portfolio page isn't working yet, why on earth would he build a link to it? It's so simple to just NOT create a link until the page is ready for viewing.

Do the links work? Do the pages load quickly? Do the pictures compliment the text? Do they fit attractively on the page? Can you read the full text without having to scroll for miles? Are there audio or video elements on the page, and do they work properly? Do they serve a purpose? Do they appeal to the site's audience?

- What can you learn from his portfolio? Most web designers include a portfolio page – a webpage that shows samples of his work. This page can be very useful to you as you try to learn about the designer's capabilities and habits. Have a look at the websites he's chosen to display, and ask the same questions about those sites that you've been asking about his. Look especially at sites that are similar to the kind of site you envision for your won business.

  If you're planning a simple informational site, have a look through his portfolio for several like that. If you're hoping to sell products on line, look for sites that include e-commerce capabilities. If you plan to use video, … you get the idea.

- Throughout the process, take notes. Make notes about the features you like and dislike, and the pages where you found them. Once you decide upon a designer, you can show him the sites you like and the ones you hate, which will be extremely valuable as he attempts to create a site that works well for your business. The more he knows about your tastes and desires, the more likely it will be that his design will satisfy your expectations.

  Also, take notes that include phone numbers. Eventually, you'll want to call a number of business owners and talk to them about their website experiences. In fact, that's Step 4 in the process.

Step 4: Talk to the Designers' Clients

A web designer's clients are your very best source of information about the designer's abilities, work habits, and customer care. You'll want to talk to several clients before you settle on the designer who will take on your website project. You might be surprised to know that most business owners are more than happy to talk about their website experiences, so don't be concerned about taking up their valuable time. Obviously, you need to be sensitive to their schedules, but if you let them know you just have a few questions, and offer to call them back at a convenient time, I think you'll find most business owners are happy to help. In fact, most people are flattered when you ask them for advice, and unless they are a direct competitor, they will gladly make time to help out a fellow entrepreneur.

But remember that the information they give you is shaded by their own unique situation. If their website is up and running and is essentially doing what they want it to do, they will probably have a favorable impression of their web designer. They may have forgotten that it took longer than they had expected it to take, or that the cost was higher than expected. It will be up to you to ask the right questions in order to get a true sense of what it would be like to work with the designer in question.

Also, bear in mind that many business owners don't realize that they've been duped, overcharged, or otherwise treated unjustly. And no one likes to admit it once they do realize it. So again, it will be up to you to ask the questions that will lead to a genuine insight into the designer's character, capabilities, and costs.

You'll want to be very sensitive to the feelings of the people you talk to. No one wants to be told that they've been cheated, so even if you come to suspect it, don't insult the guy by making him feel stupid. If you suggest to him that he's been ripped off, he will probably take on a defensive posture. He will probably justify his choices by exaggerating the quality of the service he's received from the designer you've accused of ripping him off. Putting him on the defensive will only keep him from sharing his honest experiences with you.

When you contact a business owner to talk about his website experiences, tell him you're just shopping around for a designer for your own site. Tell him you're just looking for a designer you can trust and who can do the job well. Tell him you like his website and wondered what kind of experience he'd had with getting it up and running. And then let him talk. Listen carefully for clues to the problems we've been discussing. And don't say anything that would suggest that a decision he feels good about might have been a mistake. Here are some suggested questions to get you started.

1. I don't know much about computers. I'll need somebody who can talk to me in plain English. Did you designer explain all the technical stuff to you?

2. How long did the project take? If there were delays, did you understand the causes?

3. If you call or email him with a question, do you usually hear back within a few days?

Notice that I said "a few days." In reality, your designer should respond within a few hours. A designer who can't typically respond within half a business day isn't in control of his own schedule. Either he's too busy, or he's a procrastinator. Either way, he's not your man. Everybody has days that are unusually busy, so there will be times when even the best scheduler can't respond right away. But if the typical response time is more than one business day, I'd suggest you look for someone else.

4. Were you involved in the design process? Or did he design the site and you just loved it the way he did it?

5. Were there elements that you had originally wanted that he talked you out of?

   Sometimes designers will tell clients "You don't really need that", when what they really mean is "I don't know how to do that." For some reason, geeks seem to have a very hard time admitting they don't know something. They want people to see them as brilliant technicians, and they fear that admitting they don't know everything will tarnish that reputation. Of course that's silly – No one can know everything. But my vast experience with geeks has taught me that most would rather die than utter the words "I don't know".

   I've seen many geeks make up wildly convoluted excuses for various failures in their systems. But I don't believe I've ever heard a true geek admit he didn't know the answer to a technical question.

6. Who maintains your website? Who makes changes when you need them? And how long does that take?

7. If you don't mind my asking, what did your site cost? I'm thinking of a similar design and structure for my site and I want to get a sense of what's a fair price.

8. What do you pay for hosting and maintenance? What's included in those charges?

9. Would you recommend this designer, or is there someone else I should be looking at?

   This is a really important question. I've known lots of business owners who were moderately happy with their web designer, but who later learned they could have done better. They might have an inside line on a great designer, but if you don't ask, they probably won't volunteer the information. So ask.

Step 5: Meet the Designers

Once you've looked at a wide variety of designers' websites, perused their portfolio pages, and spoken with a number of their clients, you'll be able to narrow your search to three or four finalists. If you don't have three or four viable choices, you should expand your geographic search area. Keep expanding until you have at least three good possibilities. But before you schedule appointments with them, finish reading this book. There's lots more good advice in plain English that will help you ask the right questions, and decipher the responses, so that you make the best possible decisions going forward.

Part III

The Bottom Line

CHAPTER 10

What Will Your Website Cost?

I know a lot of you have skipped ahead to this chapter. Your first concern is the bottom line, and well it should be. I know that you don't get to be a successful business owner by ignoring costs, and you're anxious to get down to the nitty gritty.

But first, I want you to understand that there are many important factors that contribute to the cost of website ownership, and the price you pay to your website designer is just one of those factors. Sometimes, that is the most important factor, but very often, it is not. Quite often, the price you pay for the design of your site is a small fraction of the overall cost of the site, so if you have skipped ahead to this chapter, take heed. The previous chapters provide insights into the world of web design that can save you a mountain of headaches, and a mountain of cash to boot.

OK, so what will a website cost? Of course, that depends upon what you want it to do, who you'll get to design it, and what arrangements you'll make for keeping it updated and working on the World Wide Web. Often, my web design clients tell me that they just need a basic website, so let's start with that.

First, we have to define what we mean by a basic website. But the definition varies from designer to designer. Some designers say they'll build you a basic site – a single page – for a set price, while others consider a basic site to be three, four, or five pages of inter-linked information. Some designers work with templates, and replace the template's text and logo with the client's text and logo. Other designers start with a blank page and build completely unique sites from scratch.

Some designers will build a site for a very low cost, expecting to make their real profits in the hosting and maintenance contracts that go with it. Others charge only for the actual design work, preferring to stay out of the hosting business altogether.

With all these variables, plus the differences in localities and cost of living indices, you can see that predicting the cost of even a "basic" site is practically impossible. A search of the Internet can provide you with some information about costs, but I caution you against accepting that information as gospel. Lots of web designers have grossly inflated their published prices so that they can offer deep discounts to help them close their deals. And others publish enticing prices for the "basic" site, then charge you an arm and a leg for every little piece of customization.

Some designers include services like proofreading and image editing in their standard pricing, while others charge an additional fee for such services. Some designers expect the client to provide the exact text and images, while others are willing to help the client tweak the wording and visuals to improve the overall effectiveness of the site. And those designers who provide that service may or may not charge extra for it.

Then there's the question about what features your site requires. Do you want buttons that change colors when you scroll over them? Or buttons that click when you click on them? Will you be publishing a newsletter? A calendar? A link to your Facebook page? Will you be accepting credit card payments online? Or providing a private login page for your clients to access their personal information? Do you want to receive emails from your website visitors? Will those need to be secure? Do you want to prevent spam from automated website snoops? Who will own your site? And who will update it?

These are just a few of the questions your designer will need to answer before he can set your price. And there are many, many more.

> Asking how much a website costs is a lot like asking how much a house costs. It depends on dozens of factors, and every website – like every house – is unique.

A website for Dan's Barber Shop will be far cheaper than a website for the Wall Street Journal. But even Dan's Barber Shop has options to consider, and questions to answer, before a designer can give him a price estimate.

Therefore, the only reasonable way to estimate your costs is to sit down with a designer and talk about your options. Show him the websites you've identified that have the features you like. Tell him how you want the site to look and what you want it to do for your business. Talk to him about how the site will be updated, and who will do the updates. And let him formulate a proposal for the job. Be sure he explains what is included in his price and what services will be extra. Ask him what his regular hourly rate is, as that will be important to you if your requirements change, or you plan for him to do your updates. Then meet with at least two more designers and get their proposals for the same job.

Once you have three written proposals, from designers whom you've already identified as trustworthy and honest, you should have a pretty good idea of what the project will cost. (See Chapter 9 for tips on identifying the good, honest designers.)

But for those of you who absolutely must have a dollar figure before you'll turn another page, I will say this: My guess is that most websites designed for local barber shops, employing fewer than 5 barbers, probably cost somewhere between $200 and $2000. Anything more specific than that would really require a conversation between the designer and the owner.

Many business owners find themselves in this situation. Maybe they built the site themselves or maybe they hired it done. And for whatever reason, they find they need to hire a designer to make some changes. It may surprise you to know that it's sometimes cheaper to start from scratch than it is to go in and try to clean up another designer's work. This isn't always the case, of course, but it is sometimes true. Your designer will be able to assess the current condition of the site and tell you what he'd charge you to make the changes you envision. Depending on the complexity of the site, the software and languages used to design it, and the extent and nature of your planned changes, the costs for editing an existing site can vary widely.

As a web designer, I'd personally much rather start from scratch than try to fix another designer's code. But if the site is extensive and the edits aren't, it makes sense to salvage the original and make it work for you. However, if the reverse is true (the site is simple and the changes are extensive), it makes more sense to scrap it and start over.

Fortunately, if you read this book carefully, you'll have the knowledge at hand that will help you negotiate a fair deal with a good designer either way.

There are two common ways of pricing a project: By the hour or by the project. If your designer charges by the hour, you'll want to keep that in mind any time you are talking to him about changes to your project. Remember that your phone calls are "on the clock", and don't let him pad the bill with conversations about the weather or your kid's soccer game. And remember that changes to the project often mean paying for work that will eventually be scrapped. Be sure you have a very clear idea of what you want before the clock starts ticking. Hourly charges rack up in a hurry if the client is indecisive.

The hourly rates charged by designers vary greatly according to the designer's expertise, location, reputation and corporate affiliations. I've seen designers who are just starting out that would work for as little as $10/hour, and corporate developers that charge well over $200/hour. The price you end up paying will depend largely on how much expertise you require of your designer. If all you need is a basic "online brochure", with no database integration or shopping cart capability, you might do well to interview some up-and-coming designers. But if you envision interactivity, or e-commerce, or Search Engine Optimization, you'll need greater expertise, and you should plan to pay for it.

The other common way of pricing websites is by the project. Designers who use this pricing scheme often charge a higher standard price, but it might save you money in the long run. If your designer proposes a price for the entire project, read the proposal carefully. Make sure it includes all the features you hope to get. Be sure the contract explains exactly what is included and what will be charged separately. If there are changes to the original work order, how will those changes be billed, and will you know the cost of those changes before the work is begun? And if the designer creates a site that you don't like, will you be charged extra for a re-design? These are important questions, and you really need to know the answers before you sign on the dotted line.

One of the most important considerations in beginning a website project (and in pricing one) is that of maintenance. Who will make changes and updates to the site once it's up and running? Deciding that ahead of time will help your designer create an appropriate structure for the site. If you are hoping to make updates yourself, or you plan to have an employee do it, be sure your designer knows that up front. Be aware, however, that a professional can often update an entire website in less time than it takes an average computer user to figure out where the files are and how to upload the changes. If your time (or the time of your employee) is worth anything, you should definitely weigh the costs. A general rule of thumb is this: If you plan to make regular updates more than once a month, you should talk to your designer about giving you editing capabilities. If, on the other hand, your site will remain essentially the same, and require just a few updates a year, you're probably better off leaving it to the professionals.

Another aspect to maintenance pricing is the possibility of negotiating a maintenance agreement with your designer. Often, designers offer substantial discounts on their usual hourly rate in exchange for a longer-term contract. For example, one company I know offers up to two hours of maintenance work per month at approximately half of their regular hourly rate. And additional hours are discounted by 25%. The client has to commit to a full year up front, but it's an attractive offer for companies that need it. So if you have a site that will have numerous changes every month, and you don't want to tie up your own time or your employees', a deal like that could prove very useful. And you have the added benefit of knowing the job will be done by a real professional who is very familiar with your site and your business.

CHAPTER 11

How Long Will it Take?

I always am amused when a web design client asks me how long it will take me to get his website finished. It seems that even clients who have been in business for years without a website, are suddenly in a big hurry to get their website up and running. But it is a fair question, and one that deserves an honest and complete answer.

By now, you realize that every website is unique, so estimating a timeframe for completing a site is impossible without some knowledge of the specific requirements of the job. Having said that, I still want you to have some idea about the completion time, so that you can know if your designer is doing his part to get the job done in a timely manner.

A simple website – a couple of basic pages, some text and pictures, without any database integration, Search Engine Optimization, custom graphics, animations, or e-commerce capability – can be designed in a few hours. But there's more to launching a website than simply designing the framework.

> The truth is, most website projects are delayed, not because the designer isn't working at it, but because *the business owner doesn't provide the content.*

Almost every website I have ever created has been delayed at one point or another because I was waiting for content from the client. This brings up an important point that you, as a business owner, must recognize. Creating a website requires input from you. Your web designer may be a genius of design and an artful communicator, but only you can know what content you need on your site.

Assume for a moment that a designer has been hired to create a website for a company that manufactures widgets. That designer can create a structure for the site, and build a basic template. He can choose a color scheme and a family of fonts that reflect his vision for the site. But he needs pictures of widgets to put on the website. And he needs some text describing what a widget is good for, why someone might want to purchase one, and why this company's widgets are better than someone else's widgets.

Typically, a client is interested in how long it will take to get the site up and running. But a better question for you to ask is this: "How much time will I be required to devote to this project?"

That's a far better question because that is the key to estimating the timeline overall.

Look at your website project one page at a time. What do you want to say on the homepage? How long will it take you to draft the paragraphs that introduce your website, your company, your products or services? What images would you like to see there? And where will those images come from?

For example, imagine that you are that widget manufacturer. Do you have quality photos of your product? Of your facilities? Of your people? What will you want to tell your website visitor on the homepage? And what pictures do you have or can you provide that will enhance the words and descriptions you put there? If you don't have good quality photos, where can you get some? Will you hire a photographer? Purchase stock images? Or will you let your designer make those decisions? Bear in mind that, if the designer procures images on your behalf, you'll be paying his marked-up price. You can usually save money by hiring a photographer yourself, rather than letting the designer hire one for you.

Go over the website plans page by page, and determine exactly what you want to accomplish on each page. You'll need to supply at least a detailed outline to your designer, and then figure out what photos will be needed to support and enhance the message of each page.

In Chapter 12, we'll discuss more specifics about what to include on your website. For now, just realize that the timeline for completing your website is in large part dependent upon your ability to supply the necessary content to your designer.

Another factor that determines how long a project will take is the designer's current workload. Like most businesses, web designers go through periods when they are very busy, and other times when things are relatively slow. If your designer is especially busy, he might not get to start your project right away. But before you sign on the dotted line, you can ask him for a basic timeline. If he's very busy, he should be able to tell you that up front, and let you know when he'll be ready to start, and roughly how long it will take – assuming he has all the content he needs from you.

Having a website project drag on for months isn't pleasant, and it happens all too often. If you are especially anxious to get your website project finished, I have a few tips to help you keep the ball rolling, and avoid unnecessary delays.

1. Tell your designer up front that time is a consideration.

2. Get your content to him. If he's waiting on you to give him something, you can hardly complain that things are taking too long.

3. Respond to every email or phone call. You don't want it to be said that any lack of communication was your fault, so be sure all of his attempts to contact you are answered.

4. Follow-up with him after you send him content. Verify that he received it and that it is complete and sufficient. Always ask if there is anything more he needs from you.

5. Touch base every couple of days. Check in on his progress - ask for updates.

6. If the project seems to be bogged down or delayed for no apparent reason, ask for an explanation. Don't forget – and don't let your designer forget - that you are a paying customer, and you expect him to live up to your agreements.

7. Be persistent and consistent. Remember, the squeaky wheel gets the grease.

Most sites can be completed within a couple of months. If after two month, your site isn't up and running and fully functional, you should understand the reason. If the delay is your own fault, talk with your designer and work up a schedule you can live with for providing content. *And then stick to it.*

If the delay is your designer's fault, let him know you expect the problems to be resolved without further delay, and stick on him until he delivers on his part of the deal.

We've all seen websites with pages that say "Under Construction", and I am forever amazed that website owners or their designers allow that to happen. Why would you want that posted on your website? If the whole site is under construction, why would you even launch it? And if a single page is under construction, why would you create a link to that page before it was ready to view?

When I see the words "Under Construction" on a web page, it tells me that the business doesn't have its act together. I might forgive it for a very brief moment, while a new page is configured to replace an old one, for example. But a website that posts those words for more than a day, is not doing its owners any favors. Incomplete websites, and sites with links that don't work right, are bad advertising. They tell visitors that the business is inept or careless or incompetent or worse. Please don't let your designer do that to you.

Your website is your corporate image. When you leave it "under construction" for days and weeks on end, it portrays an image of your business that is counter to its purpose. If you genuinely believe you must post a placeholder, let me suggest one like this one for Willy Nilly's Widgets.

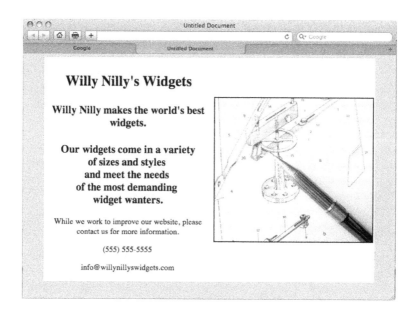

At least this tells the visitor something useful about your business. It's still a poor excuse for a functional website, but it's better than some cheesy picture of hard hats in a construction zone. Those were cute in 1995. They are just tiresome now.

So how long does it take to build a website? It depends on how complex the site is, how busy the designer is with other projects, and how quickly the client can assemble the content. But, as a general rule, I'd suggest that, if your site that isn't finished within two months, someone isn't doing his job. In that case, you should have an honest conversation with your designer to determine where the bottleneck is, and what needs to happen to clear it.

CHAPTER 12

What to Include on Your Site

You have already decided you need a website, but maybe you're not sure what to put on it. You have some ideas, and you've looked around at other websites, but you're uncertain how much information to put out there, or which images will work best for your business. So what should you include – and what should you omit – when you're piecing together your corporate website? Well, that depends.

It depends upon the kind of business you're in and the overall purpose of your website. It also depends upon your budget as most website designers charge, at least in part, by the page. And it depends upon your target market and what your customers will find useful and appealing.

A good rule of thumb, when deciding what to include in a website, is to remember that the consumer of this product is actually your website visitor, and the contents of the site are there for their benefit. Any content you place on your site needs to fulfill a mission, solve a problem, provide useful information, encourage further contact, or promote your business, products, services and people. If you're considering placing something on your website and you're not sure it belongs there, ask yourself which of those purposes it serves. If it serves none of those purposes, it probably doesn't belong on your corporate website.

Having said that, I want to express to you that there are many things that aren't immediately related to your business that you might still want to post on your website. For example, if you sponsor a Little League team, it might be appropriate to post a picture of the team on your site. Probably not on the homepage, but we can probably find a good spot for that. Or if you have an employee who was recently awarded some big honor, by all means, post that on your site. The truth is that almost any positive news you can post about your employees is good public relations, and that's one of the purposes of a corporate website. People like to know that your business cares about its employees. And it's usually good for employee morale, too.

Every website is unique and every business is unique. So laying down rules about what should or shouldn't be included in a website would be a futile exercise. But I think it might be helpful for the very newest website owners to consider what should go on each of the basic pages that almost every website includes:

- The Home page
- The About Us page
- The Products/Services page
- The Contact Us page

I believe that above all, the homepage must be simple for the visitor to understand. In my own website design business, we use the tag line *"Simply Brilliant!"* not just because I am simply brilliant, but because I have developed a design philosophy centered around the brilliance of simplicity. When you think about the world's most recognizable logos – the Nike swoosh, or the Pepsi wave, or the little apple with the chunk out of it – you realize that they are powerful emblems because they are simple. And I believe that a website – especially a homepage – is most powerful when it is simple.

Let's face it, if your homepage is cluttered and confusing and the buttons are difficult to maneuver, your website isn't going to sell anybody anything. People don't want a challenge when they come to your website. People want information. That's why I believe the purpose of the homepage is to tell a visitor: Yes, this is the site you were looking for (or No, it's not the site you were looking for). And it should be blatantly obvious where they need to click to get the information they came for.

And the second purpose of the homepage is to give the visitor a positive first impression of your business. My philosophy about homepage design is that it should be more like a billboard than a newspaper. When the page opens, I want the visitor to instantly approve of the overall appeal of the site, because you only get one chance to make that first impression. If a visitor opens your homepage and it presents a positive image, and it presents a simple path to the information he came to find, the homepage has accomplished its mission. Other pages can present the details, as long as the path to those pages is apparent from the homepage.

Not every designer agrees with this assessment, as is evident at websites all over the Internet. But I hold up the Google homepage as evidence that simplicity is a powerful tool when properly implemented.

So, on your homepage, I recommend a very brief statement about who you are and what you do. Include some high quality photos because web surfers like pictures. And move the details back to another page.

About Us

This page is a place to put all kinds of information about your business. This need not be as simple as the homepage, but it stills needs to be laid out logically and attractively. Some of the things you might consider for this page include:

- Your mission statement
- Your business philosophy
- A brief history of your business
- An overview of your business model
- Brief bios of the business owners
- Photos of your people, facilities or products

- What makes your company better than the competition

- Human-interest stories (like the Little League team you sponsor or the charities you support).

This page is an empty slate that you can decorate with anything that will reflect positively on your business. Have some fun with it and give your business a human face.

Products/Services

As the name implies, this is the page you use to describe your products and services. Depending upon the kind of business you are in, you may need extra pages to describe all of the products or services your company sells. If that's the case, I recommend this page be used to display an overview or summary, and then provide links to the detail pages. As on all web pages, the quality of the photos you choose to display is key to presenting a clear, professional image of your business and your products.

Contact Us

This page is important for every website, because all web visitors expect you to have a contact page. (By the way, they also expect the link to that page to be found at the very last position in the navigation bar. If your navigation buttons run vertically along the edge of the page, the bottom button should link to your contact page. And if your navigation runs horizontally, the contact button should be the last one on the far right.)Your contact page should be simple, and should avoid small fonts so that people can easily dial your phone number or copy your address without eye strain. You should include all of the following on your contact page:

- Your physical address
- Your mailing address (if it's different from your physical address)
- Your phone number
- Your Fax number
- Your email address
- An email form like the one shown below. This is helpful for the visitor who uses webmail like Yahoo or Gmail to send and receive email. Without the form, he would have to copy your email address, login to his webmail, and paste the address into a message. With a web form, he just enters his name and email address and his comments, then clicks send. You'll receive an email either way and you can then email him back to respond to his inquiry.

| Your Name: | |
| Your email: | |

Comments:

[   ]

SEND

How Much is Too Much?

If you have more information you want to share with your visitors, you can add more pages. But I caution you against putting too much text on a single page. Your website visitors will be annoyed if they have to scroll for miles to get to the bottom of your page. Instead, I recommend you follow the Rule of Three, which limits a page's content to the area of roughly three screen sizes. In other words, when a visitor opens your webpage, his browser should be able to display approximately one-third of the page's content at once. If your web pages are longer than that, consider splitting them into smaller chucks.

Your web designer may charge you by the page, and you may be tempted, therefore, to cram more data onto a single page. Don't do it. The resulting pages will be poorly accepted by your visitors and will affect their impression of your company. Always remember these words:

Your website is your corporate image.

Make it Brilliant, and keep it Simple.

Simply Brilliant!

Part IV

E-Commerce

CHAPTER 13

E-Commerce Websites

E-commerce is simply the sale of products and services over the Internet. If you've ever purchased a product and paid for it online, you've been a participant in e-commerce. Online banking, auctions, and music download sites are also examples of e-commerce sites. If you are considering selling your products or services online, and plan to accept credit card or PayPal payments, you'll need an e-commerce website. But you may be wondering what makes an e-commerce site different from a plain old static website. The answer, as you might have guessed, depends upon the purpose, scale, and scope of the commerce you plan to do there. But there is one thing that almost all e-commerce sites contain, so I'll start with a discussion of the e-commerce cornerstone, a software program called the shopping cart.

Most e-commerce sites include some form of shopping cart – a program that keeps track of all the items a visitor chooses to buy from your site. The shopping cart holds onto the items' information (price, quantity, color, etc.) until the visitor proceeds to the "checkout". You might think that the shopping cart handles the whole transaction, but actually, it only serves to pass the item information on to the payment gateway. (We'll talk about payment gateways shortly.)

You'll need to purchase a shopping cart, and getting the right one for your purposes is crucial. There are dozens – maybe hundreds – of packages to choose from, so it might help to talk to your designer about exactly what you want the shopping cart to do and how you expect it to function. A high-end shopping cart can cost upwards of $1000, but it might be that you don't need all the features of a high-end package. In fact, you may find a good package that meets your needs for $250 - $400. But be very careful about your choice. Changing down the road from one shopping cart to another completely different one can be a time-consuming, costly process. You may think you only need certain features for now, but think about the future. Make sure you leave yourself plenty of room for expansion.

A good shopping cart program will include dozens of very sophisticated features that will help you and your customers avoid problems and mistakes. In fact, shopping carts have become so sophisticated, they can actually be your entire website. In addition to static pages about your business and your staff, for example, they can include a wide range of functions designed to increase your sales and streamline the processes. I describe a few of these functions below, but there are many, many more.

May we also suggest… Your shopping cart program may include a feature that suggests additional products to complement a customer's current selection. Designed to increase impulse buying, this strategy can prove highly successful, especially if it's combined with a discount.

Quantity Discounts and Coupons. Many shopping carts can calculate discount rates based on the number of units a customer wishes to purchase. Coupon functions are a great way to entice visitors to your site. In your email or other marketing, you can give your customers special codes that are matched against a particular item or overall discount rate. When they enter the code during checkout, the discount is automatically applied.

Tax and Shipping Calculators. Most shopping cart programs incorporate calculators that will apply the correct sales tax and shipping costs, based on the address of the customer, the local tax rate, and the shipping method they select. If you are selling a service that isn't subject to sales tax, you can configure the program to reflect that as well.

Newsletter integration. Today, many shopping carts integrate with Constant Contact or other newsletter programs, while others include a newsletter function of their own. These can be powerful marketing tools, so look for a package that includes this feature.

Other common features include product reviews, wish lists, and inventory tracking. But there's more to choosing a shopping cart than just getting the features you need. Before you purchase a software package, you'll need to answer these questions:

What will it cost? Be careful that you don't bust your budget on a shopping cart package and forget to include the peripheral costs. You'll also need a payment gateway (discussed below), and if the program is very complex, you may well need to pay for someone to help you set up and configure shopping cart.

What programming languages does my hosting service support? Shopping cart scripts are written in many different programming languages. Be sure to check with your hosting provider before you buy any shopping cart. If you choose a remotely hosted service, then it won't matter what programming language the cart software is written in. I'll tell you more about remotely hosted services shortly.

Does the shopping cart allow for scalability? Think about where your business might be a year or two down the road. As your business grows, you may find that your e-commerce needs change. Many shopping carts are sold in a modular format that allows for scalability. This is very helpful, because replacing a whole shopping cart system can be a painful and costly endeavor. But don't get swindled. Some companies will offer the base model at a very low price, then charge enormous prices for the upgrades and add-on modules. If you plan to purchase a modular package, be sure you take the price of the add-ons into consideration.

Is the cart software compatible with my payment gateway? A payment gateway is an e-commerce service that authorizes online credit card payments. It is typically associated with the online store's a merchant account. There are many different payment gateways, and they each work with a number of shopping cart packages - but maybe not the shopping cart you've chosen. Before purchasing your cart, be sure it is compatible with your gateway. (Also make sure that the payment gateway is compatible with the Internet merchant account you have with your bank.)

What about disaster planning? Your shopping cart application should have comprehensive support for backing up files and allowing for export into a variety of formats. (The ability to export your files will also be of value in the future if you ever need to change carts and need to import your existing data into a new application.)

What kind of support will I need and will it be readily – and affordably - available? All shopping cart providers will tell you that their software is simple to install and configure. But please don't believe them. Unless you have the technical expertise to configure your shopping cart, you'll need to get quotes from the company or a third party contractor to undertake this work for you. And if you do have expertise, you still need to ask yourself if you have the time to do it yourself. Experience has taught me that configuring and customizing a shopping cart can consume many, many hours, and access to good technical support is almost always needed.

It's a good idea to test out the support system by sending a query to the sales department - if they don't respond quickly, you can probably assume that any after-sales support will be even worse.

Also, be aware that technical support is often charged out per incident. So read the fine print and know what you're getting before you buy.

Should I buy a remotely hosted shopping cart or a locally hosted one? Shopping cart programs can be purchased as stand alone programs, which live on your own server, or as pay per month services hosted on another companies' server. As you probably guessed, there are advantages and disadvantages to both types.

Remote hosting advantages

Remotely hosted shopping carts, as a general rule, offer their own secure connection, monitoring of service, and usually many other features are offered as part of the service. Also, if your products are soft goods that are delivered via downloads, a remotely hosted cart can save you money on bandwidth charges.

Some remotely hosted shopping carts offer a complete e-commerce solution, combining the shopping cart program with gateway services and even an Internet merchant account!

If you need to find a solution that doesn't entail a large investment of funds up front, a remotely hosted cart may well be your best bet. You'll probably spend at least $100 per month for these kinds of services. But shop around carefully, as prices and features vary substantially from one vendor to another.

Remote hosting disadvantages

The worst-case scenario might be if the company hosting your shopping cart goes out of business. If you are going to use a remotely hosted service, check the company history carefully. And get some assurance that they will never 'harvest' or sell your client databases.

Local hosting advantages

The big advantage to a locally hosted shopping cart is that you are in full control over the software, and that once you pay for the software, there are no monthly charges to maintain it. Of course, you'll still have your hosting charges, and the additional monthly charge for a Secure Sockets Layer (SSL), but they should be substantially less than the monthly fee for a remotely hosted cart.

Local hosting disadvantages

Probably the largest deterrent to the locally hosted shopping cart is the initial cost of the software – often thousands of dollars. But another major drawback is the time you'll spend (or pay someone else to spend) on installation, configuration and maintenance.

Free or premium shopping carts?

It's very important before you begin reviewing software and services to be to be very specific in what you actually want the cart to be able to do. You might determine that you really don't need all the bells and whistles offered by high end packages. If this is the case, then you can probably find a decent program for around $250 - $300. Some companies offer free shopping carts, but be sure to read the fine print. Sometimes there are hidden costs that can really add up .

Be careful not to limit yourself . Look for a package that can grow with your business. You may only want limited features at first, but what about in the future? Make sure your software has the flexibility you may need in the future. You definitely don't want to have to change software mid-stream once you have one shopping cart already built.

Free ecommerce solutions

One of the best free e-commerce solutions available to you is Paypal, which combines basic shopping cart functions with a payment gateway and merchant account. It is free to set it up, and you pay only a per-transaction fee. (As of this writing, the transaction fee is about 3% of the sale plus 30 cents per transaction.) PayPal is an excellent way to begin in e-commerce and is commonly accepted and trusted around the world.

I should alert you to a couple of disadvantages to using PayPal, however. First, your funds are paid to you via check or through direct deposit, but it sometimes takes a few days for that transaction to get processed, so you don't get your money right away. And secondly, because PayPal subtracts their fees from the check amount, your deposit amounts don't match up precisely with your sales transaction amounts. When you are trying to balance your books, this can be a real pain as you attempt to marry up your sales receipts and your deposits.

Still, the simplicity of the setup and the public trust associated with PayPal are reasonably strong incentives for considering it as a viable choice for your payment gateway. Visit the PayPal website (www.paypal.com) for current pricing and available features.

Some final thoughts

Obviously, there are a lot of things to consider when you decide to open an online store. But it's critically important that you do your homework before you begin. Especially when it comes to selecting a shopping cart, you really can't rush the decision, because changing your mind later on will be time-consuming and costly. And the interruption of service could prove costly or even fatal to your business.

So take your time and compare your options. Talk to the sales reps of several companies. Formulate a clear plan of where you want to go and how you want to get there.

Most of the best companies offer a 30-day money back guarantee. Use your 30 days to really learn the programs, test them out, and put the support team through some paces. Then, if you're not really happy, dump it and go elsewhere. It's far better to begin again after 30 days than it will be to live with a unsatisfactory situation for years to come.

A full comparison of available shopping cart packages is beyond the scope of this book, but a number of reviews and technical reports have been published online. A Google search of "shopping cart reviews" would be a good place to start.

Part V

Driving Visitors to Your Site

CHAPTER 14

Finding Your Site on Google

One of the first questions most business owners have about their website is "How can I make sure people can find my site?" For most businesses, this is a critically important question. You need to know that, once your website is up and running, your customers and potential customers will see it. I'm sure you've heard the famous quote from my all-time favorite movie, *Field of Dreams*: "If you build it, they will come." Unfortunately, that's not necessarily true when it comes to websites. The reality is that you might build a truly beautiful, technically sweet, visually powerful, and immensely compelling website, but building it doesn't mean people will come to it. You have to drive them there.

Driving traffic to your website is every bit as important as building a good site, and this section of the book is all about helping you do that. We'll begin by discussing ways to make your website "Search Engine Friendly", and how to optimize the site so that it gets the highest possible rankings on Google and the other search engines. But let's start with a few basic definitions.

A **search engine** is a tool designed to search for information on the Internet. Google is an example of a search engine, but there are many others as well. Throughout this chapter, and the rest of the book, I'll use Google as my example search engine. Unless I tell you otherwise, you can assume that what I tell you about Google is also true of the majority of the other search engines commonly in use in the United States.

SERP stands for Search Engine Results Page and, as the name implies, that is the web page that displays the results of a user's search. Let's say, for example, that you went to Google and typed the words "bowling shoes" into the search box and pressed Enter. Google would find a list of websites that are related to bowling shoes in one way or another. There would likely be companies listed there that sell bowling shoes, and companies that manufacture bowling shoes. There might be bowling alleys listed that rent bowling shoes, and maybe a bowler's bar called "Bowling Shoes Bar and Grill". There might be other pages listed there whose only connection to bowling shoes is that they posted a blog that mentioned that someone just bought a pair of bowling shoes. The point is, that Google locates websites that are somehow related to the words you searched for, and they post them on a new webpage called a SERP. Throughout this book, I'll often refer to a SERP as a results page. For our purposes, the two terms are synonymous.

The **SERP rank** of a web page refers to the placement of the corresponding link on the SERP, where higher placement means higher SERP rank. The SERP rank of a web page is determined by complex algorithm involving a large and continuously adjusted set of factors. We'll talk about what some of those factors are later in this chapter. It is common to see the terms SERP rank and PageRank used interchangeably. But **PageRank** is actually the patented algorithm, named after Larry Page, a co-founder of Google. This algorithm is used by Google to measure the relative importance of various web pages, in relation to each other and to the words entered in the search.

You might like to know...

The name "PageRank" is a trademark of Google, and the PageRank process has been patented (U.S. Patent 6,285,999). However, the patent is assigned to Stanford University and not to Google. Google purchased exclusive license rights on the patent from Stanford University. The university reportedly received 1.8 million shares of Google, and sold those shares in 2005 for a handsome $336 Million.

SEO (Search Engine Optimization) is the science behind improving a website's SERP rank. Obviously, you'd like your website to have the highest possible ranking on Google, and that's what this chapter is all about.

My first bit of advice regarding SEO is to determine how important Internet traffic is to your business. If you believe that it's very important, you need to hire an SEO company before you build your website. The cost is substantial –$3000 and up, depending on the complexity of the site - but if the SERP rank of your website is very important to you, and the success of your business depends upon it, you really need to accept that this is one expense you simply can't forego. If your website is the lifeblood of your business, and you expect to make tens of thousands of dollars a year (or more) from that business, then please invest a few thousand in SEO and assure the best possible SERP rank.

By contrast, if your business is not reliant upon website traffic to bring you customers, you might logically decide to spend your marketing budget elsewhere, and not hire an SEO company. That's not to say you don't need a good SERP rank, however, so please keep reading.

Unless you hire an SEO company to optimize your website from the ground up, you'll be relying upon your web designer to create a website that is, at the very least, "search engine friendly". That means that the design of the site makes it easy for Google and other search engines to "crawl" around your site and gather information about the content of your site. There are many steps any designer can take to help a site become search engine friendly, and you should talk to your designer about which of those steps he'll be taking on your behalf.

Making Your Site SEO Friendly

There are a number of factors to consider in the creation of your site that can make or break the search engine friendliness of the site. The main thing to keep in mind throughout this chapter is that Google is looking for "keywords", the words a user types into the search field on the Google website. Everything we are about to discuss is geared toward getting those keywords out there where Google can find them.

The example site I've chosen is a fictitious business called Joe's Bike Shop, where Joe sells and repairs bicycles. The first step is to determine which keywords Joe needs to target. Later, we'll talk about ways to use those keywords throughout the website to maximize their effectiveness, but first we have to figure out what those keywords are.

Joe comes up with a list of possible keywords – words he imagines his customers would enter into a search field if they were trying to find his website. And he comes up with a few:

bike, bike shop, bike repair, Joe's Bike Shop, bike store, bike accessories, and bike parts.

This is a start, but if you search for the words "bike shop" on Google, you might well get a page full of websites for motorcycle enthusiasts. Joe needs those keywords on his site, because users might very well choose them when looking for his store. But he also needs to target the same phrases using the word bicycle instead of bike. Now his list is:

bike, bike shop, bike repair, Joe's Bike Shop, bike store, bike accessories, bike parts, bicycle, bicycle shop, bicycle repair, Joe's Bicycle Shop, bicycle store, bicycle accessories, bicycle parts.

But many of Joe's customers are serious cycling enthusiasts, so they might use that word instead of bicycle:

bike, bike shop, bike repair, Joe's Bike Shop, bike store, bike accessories, bike parts, bicycle, bicycle shop, bicycle repair, Joe's Bicycle Shop, bicycle store, bicycle accessories, bicycle parts, cycle, cycle shop, cycle repair, Joe's Cycle Shop, cycle store, cycle accessories, cycle parts.

The list is getting long, and there's still an important factor missing – location. If you Googled "bicycle shop", you might get results for shops a thousand miles away. So you'd be forced to narrow your search, right? So Joe needs to add locations to his keywords:

bike, bike shop, bike repair, Joe's Bike Shop, bike store, bike accessories, bike parts, bicycle, bicycle shop, bicycle repair, Joe's Bicycle Shop, bicycle store, bicycle accessories, bicycle parts, cycle, cycle shop, cycle repair, Joe's Cycle Shop, cycle store, cycle accessories, cycle parts, bikes in Smallville, bike shop in Smallville, bike repair in Smallville, Joe's Bike Shop in Smallville, bike store in Smallville, bike accessories in Smallville, bike parts in Smallville, bicycle in Smallville, bicycle shop in Smallville, bicycle repair in Smallville, Joe's Bicycle Shop in Smallville, bicycle store in Smallville, bicycle accessories in Smallville, bicycle parts in Smallville, cycle in Smallville, cycle shop in Smallville, cycle repair in Smallville, Joe's Cycle Shop in Smallville, cycle store in Smallville, cycle accessories in Smallville, cycle parts in Smallville.

OK, so he's now targeting customers in Smallville, but what about those customers in nearby Biggerville? And throughout Middlesize County? More keywords. And what about the guy who just needs new tires for his bike or a new helmet? Should he add "Bike tires in Smallville"? Or "bicycle tires in Biggerville" ? Or "Cycle helmets in Middlesize County"? And what if the customer misspells a word? "Bycycle" is a fairly common misspelling. Should Joe also target poor spellers? And plural versions? And additional product lines? The answer to all of these is a firm and unwavering maybe. Whether or not you target those keywords, and how much you target them will depend upon their importance to your marketing strategy. A good SEO company has the tools and the expertise to do the actual research to determine which keywords are the most powerful and will most likely result in website visitors and actual sales. Without them, you'll just have to give it your best guess.

Now that Joe has settled on a list of keywords, he hands the list over to his web designer, who incorporates those words into Joe's website. He first places the very best of these keywords in the header code – a section of the HTML code that site visitors can't see, but that Google can see. Then he incorporates them throughout the content of the pages of Joe's site. Using your top keywords throughout the actual content of your pages is very powerful when it comes to your SERP rank. Google really loves content.

The designer will also use selected keywords in the page titles and the navigation links, which is another indication to Google that these words are important. If your designer is using Flash to create your navigation buttons, he should include a text version of the navigation at the bottom of your pages. That's because Google can't read the Flash buttons. I discuss Flash in more detail shortly.

A site map is another element your designer can add to enhance your search engine friendliness. This is a page that includes a list of all the pages on your web site. Site maps can be useful for your site visitors, but they are especially useful to web crawlers like the ones that Google uses to sniff out pertinent content on your site.

Each webpage on your site has what is called a header, a block of HTML code that is invisible to the website visitor, but that includes important information that browsers need in order to display the pages properly. Google reads the header code and searches for keywords, so it's important for your designer to include your keywords in the "meta tags" that are found in the header. In addition to the list of keywords, he should also include a page title and a description, as well as other meta tags that he may deem appropriate.

A Few Words About Flash

While many of the very coolest websites have beautiful and creatively awesome navigation buttons, most of those buttons are completely invisible to Google. Buttons that change colors, spin, shrink, or morph into alien creatures, are usually created in Flash, and all Flash is essentially invisible to Google. It's cool, and it's fun, and it has its place, but Google can't read it, so it does nothing for your SERP rank.

That's an important point so let me dress it up and shout it out loud.

> # Flash is essentially invisible to Google.

Oh, sorry, did someone say, "What's Flash"? Flash is a program that has become a very popular method for adding animation and interactivity to web pages. When you see slideshows, animations, or dynamic navigation buttons on a website, there's a good chance it's Flash. So when you are planning your website design, just remember that as cool as they can be, all those Flash elements do nothing to get Google's attention.

If your entire site is built in Flash – and many sites are – it is practically impossible to gain the top SERP ranks. My recommendation is to limit your use of Flash elements to specific areas of a page, and remember that whatever you are showing there is invisible to the search engines like Google.

Submitting Your Site to Google

Once you have your site built, it's a good idea to submit it to a number of search engines. Which search engines you choose to submit to depends upon your time and your budget, as some search engines charge you for the privilege. Submitting to Google is free, and very easy. Just go to www.google.com/addurl, where you'll complete a simple form. To find other search engines that allow for free submissions, just Google "free website submission", or ask your designer.

Some sites require more information about you and your business before you can submit, and the process can take some time. If your designer offers this as a service, you might consider paying him to do it. Because he'll be more familiar with the processes and the websites, he'll be able to do it much more quickly than you can, but you'll have to pay for him the service. It largely depends upon what your own time is worth.

SEO Tidbits

The PageRank algorithm is so complex and involves so many constantly evolving factors, that it's impossible to create a perfect site that will always end up with the top ranking. I can't go into all of these factors, but there are a few I want to talk to you about so you can bear them in mind as you and your designer proceed through your website project.

Reciprocal links. One of the factors Google considers when assessing the relative importance of a website is how many other sites link to it. If your web designer puts a link on his own webpage that links to your site, that will help. If CNN puts your link on their site, it would help a lot more. That's because CNN's website is assessed by Google to be a more important site than your web designer's site. Still, ask your designer, and your other business associates, to link to your website from their own sites. In return, you can link to their sites and it will benefit both businesses.

Visitor counts. Another factor that Google considers is the number of visitors and how long they stay on each page. So when you first launch your website, send the URL to your friends and family. Ask them to look over the site carefully, checking for typos and other errors. That will not only help you proofread your pages, it will start to show Google that you have traffic. It won't make a huge difference in your SERP rank, but it sure won't hurt. While you're at it, ask them to bookmark your page. That helps too because Google considers how many people have bookmarked your webpages as well.

And finally…

I really want to stress the value of hiring a good SEO company to speed the process along. While the expense is not trivial, especially to a young start-up business, the results can mean the difference between success and failure – especially if your business truly depends upon Internet traffic. If that's the case, you can't afford not to have a solid SEP company in your court. In fact, I would venture to say that, when Internet traffic is crucial, the best SEO companies don't cost you money – they make you money.

CHAPTER 15

Marketing Your Website

Search Engine Optimization can definitely help drive traffic to your website, but there are other powerful strategies that you can and should use that can bring new and existing customers to your website. Just placing your website on the World Wide Web isn't enough. You have to actively market your website while you market your business.

Driving Traffic Through Advertising

One very good way to drive traffic to your website is through your advertising and other marketing tools. Always include your URL - the address of your website – in any printed advertising you do. Your business cards, brochures, flyers and newspaper ads should all include the URL. Even your business forms – letterhead, invoice forms, etc. – should include your Internet address. But that's just the beginning. You also have to give people a reason to go there.

Let's assume, for example, that Joe's Bike Shop ran the following ad in the local paper:

Joes Bike Shop

Bikes, Parts and Repairs

Everything for the Cycling Enthusiast

(555) 555-5555

www.joesamazingbikes.com

Let's compare that to the following ad:

Joes Bike Shop

Bikes, Parts and Repairs

Everything for the Cycling Enthusiast

(555) 555-5555

Visit our website for money saving coupons

www.joesamazingbikes.com

Now he's given people a reason to check out his website. And that is the key. Print advertising is expensive and very limited. You can only tell people what you can fit in the space you can afford. But once you get them to your website, you can show them your full sales presentation, samples of your products and services, anything! You're not limited by space or time. Your website is your whole business – your products, services, people, facilities, policies, philosophies, everything! And it's all there - online - for your customers to see and assess. The key is getting them to your website in the first place. So whenever and wherever possible, give them a reason to go.

Incentives can come in a variety of forms. Joe's money-saving coupons are just one example. You might run a contest or a sweepstakes. Your site might include helpful tips or educational information relating to your products and services. Or you might lure in visitors through the online networking media like Twitter and Facebook. We'll talk more about those venues in Chapter 16.

Email Advertising

Another powerful tool for driving traffic to your website is the use of email advertising campaigns like Constant Contact. The beauty of these tools is that it reaches your customers while they are already at their computer. If the ad you send includes information they are interested in, it's really easy for them to just click on a link and be on your website instantly.

There are lots of email marketing companies available to you, so I encourage you to shop around. I don't have personal knowledge of most of them, but I am very familiar with Constant

Contact, which has long been the leader in the field of email marketing. Because I am familiar with their products and services, I'll use them as an example. But similar services are offered by a number of other companies, so it might be worth your time to investigate other offerings.

Constant Contact allows you to use email to market your business, and stay in touch with your customers and potential customers.

They provide hundreds of professionally designed templates that you can use to create beautiful newsletters and email promotions. These templates are very customizable, so you can create the look and feel that works best for your business and your customers.

They manage your email lists so you don't have to. You can import your existing email addresses to your Constant Contact mailing lists, and add a button to your website that encourages visitors to "Join our mailing list". When a visitor clicks there, he completes a very brief form and their information is automatically added to your mailing list.

You can send out as many mailings as you want without paying extra. Your charges are based on the number of addresses in your mailing list – not on the number of emails you send.

Constant Contact provides great tracking and reporting for your mailings. You can see how many were delivered, how many bounced back undeliverable, how many were deleted without opening, how many were forwarded and to whom, and much more. And my personal favorite feature is the peace of mind they provide because they are on top of the legal issues. Every email you send through Constant Contact includes the ability to opt out (unsubscribe), so you won't get into hot water over spamming regulations.

There's a lot more that a company like Constant Contact can do for your business, and the price is very reasonable. (As of this writing, the price for a mailing list of up to 500 names was just $15/month, and that includes all the templates and other features I just described. The price goes up as your mailing list grows. But if you have over 500 names on a list of people who have requested your mailings, that's a great problem to have!

Pay-Per-Click

Another form of advertising for your website is through Pay-Per-Click (PPC). If you wee to advertise on via PPC system, your company would be allowed to place ads on another company's website. You would only have to pay the host company when a visitor clicked on your ad. Several PPC providers exist, but Google AdSense is one of the largest, so again, I'll use them as an example. And I'll bring Joe's Bike Shop back to complete the illustration.

Let's assume that Joe wanted to advertise his business via Google AdSense. He would sign an agreement with Google that would allow his ads to run on the Google website or on the websites of Google's other clients. Joe would select the keywords he wanted to target and would set a monthly budget for his Google advertising.

Now this is where the scenario can get confusing. Joe sets a budget. That is, he tells Google how much he's willing to pay each month for the clicks he receives. So let's assume Joe agrees to pay $100/month for his clicks. How many clicks would that earn him? Well, that depends upon what other businesses are also paying for PPC on those same keywords, and how much they set as their monthly budget. In essence, Joe is bidding for clicks against all the other businesses that want to use PPC and target the same keywords Joe has chosen.

The numbers are very hard to predict. Even Google won't predict how many clicks you'll get or even how many visitors will be shown your ad. They only promise that the higher your monthly budget, the more clicks you'll get. But let's move on. The whole scheme will become clearer as you understand more of the moving part.

Now Joe's Bike Shop has ads that can run on other websites, and Google determines which websites that will be. Google tries to match up advertisers like Joe with host websites that have similar content. And one of the websites they identify is a website for a cross-country bike race, called BikeTrek2000. The idea here is that visitors who are interested in a bike race might also be interested in what Joe has to offer. So Google runs Joe's ad on the BikeTrek2000 website (and other sites as well). And if a visitor clicks on Joe's ad, Joe's website will appear in their browser. Joe would then pay a portion of his budget for that click, and Google would share those proceeds with BikeTrek2000.

That is a very simplified explanation of how PPC works. To better understand it, and to get a sense of how well it might work for your business, I can only suggest that you read all about it on the Google website. Just go to google.com and click on "Advertising Programs". Then if you're interested, you can sign up for a trial period, set a modest budget, and see how it goes.

The flip side of Google AdSense is called Google AdWords. In our example, Joe's Bike Shop has signed up for Google AdSense and will pay Google for clicks on their ads. On the other end of the transaction is BikeTrek2000 who is a Google AdWords participant. BikeTrek2000 has agreed to display ads on their website in exchange for a percentage of the proceeds.

A Note of Caution

I want to raise a note of caution about AdWords and similar programs that may seem appealing to you. If you put yourself in the shoes of BikeTrek2000, you might not be too excited about running other people's ads on your website. You would only get paid if your visitor clicks on the ad, and that would result in their being taken away from your website. It seems to me that there are very few commercial websites that would benefit from such an arrangement. If you have visitors on your site, your goal should be to keep them there until they have purchased something, or contacted you, or found all the information they needed from your site. Inviting them to click away to someone else's website seems counterproductive at best, and if the ad they clicked on belonged to a competitor, that would be the worst possible outcome.

CHAPTER 16

Web 2.0

You may or may not have heard the term "Web 2.0", and if you have heard it, you may not know what it means. Let me assure you that you are not alone. There isn't, as yet, a definition that has been universally accepted, but there is a common sense of what it means. The term might imply that there's a new version of the Internet appearing on the horizon, but it's not a technical upgrade or improved hardware. Web 2.0 refers to a change in the way we use the Internet, and how we interact with it.

Web 2.0 is less about static informational websites and more about interactivity. Ten years ago, we looked to the internet for basic information, but today we look to it to enhance our lives, enrich our relationships, and intensify the possibilities. Web 2.0 is just the latest ripple in the pond.

To illustrate the meaning of the term, lets view a few examples of what the world now calls Web 2.0.

Social Networking Websites

Websites like Facebook, Twitter, and LinkedIn have dramatically changed the way many people work, study, communicate, and recreate. These sites allow friends, families, colleagues, and total strangers to interact in ways that have not been possible in the past.

These sites have taken on enormous followings, and Americans of all demographics are participating. It seems that almost everyone of employment age is enrolled in at least one of these networks. If you, as a business leader, aren't working at least one of these sites, I strongly encourage you to get started. It's free, it's easy to do, and if you put some time and thought into it, I believe it will help you grow your business.

Blogs

The term "blog" is short for "web log", and has become the writer's journal for the 21st century. But it can be more than just a personal journal. It's a place to post your ideas and let the world respond. It's also a place for a private conversation between just two people. Anyone with a thought to share can post a blog on the Internet, and offer it up for the world to see. And most blogging sites allow you to share photos as well.

For more information about blogging, visit some of the more common blog sites. Blogger.com is enormously popular and full of fun and interactive features.

Wikis

A **wiki** is a website that allows its visitors to create and edit its content using any browser. The most recognizable example of a wiki is Wikipedia, a collaborative encyclopedia where any visitor can post articles or edit existing articles. (Yes, you could go in there and change Abraham Lincoln's birth date or the winner of the 1999 World Series. So take anything you read there with a grain of salt.)

Getting Visitors to Your Site – Summing It Up

So go out there and get started. Build a site that's search engine friendly, target the right keywords and use them in your content, submit your site to a number of search engines, set up reciprocal links, get your friends involved, and then market your website when you market your business. And incorporate some Web 2.0 into your website and into your life. Over time, these steps will definitely help improve your SERP rank as well as your visitor count, and ultimately your bottom line.

Part VI

Other Stuff

A Few Choice Links

The following links have been provided because I thought they might prove helpful to you, my fellow small business owners.

Emcie Media: emcie.com

websites-4smallbusiness.us

twitter.com

facebook.com

linkedin.com

constantcontact.com

myfax.com

localendar.com

paypal.com

payjunction.com

google.com

merchantcircle.com

manta.com

ratemyhost.com

About the Author

Marianne Carlson graduated *Summa cum Laude* in 1997 from the University of Maryland (European Division) with a BS in Information Systems Management. Since then, she has managed a diverse career in Information Technology and Web Design.

She served as the Computer Support and Training Coordinator for the Vermont Judiciary, where she managed a team of 18 Power Users who led the Judiciary through the challenging transition from "dumb terminal" computing era into the world of personal computers. In 2000, the Power User team, under Marianne's leadership, was honored as a State of Vermont Outstanding Team for Public Service, the only team from the Judicial Branch to receive such an honor.

September 11, 2001 was a defining moment in her life. Although she had no close friends lost in the terrorist attacks that day, she was deeply moved by the patriotism that embraced the nation, and she felt a new and powerful sense of national pride and commitment. She vowed, "If my country ever needed me, I would be proud to serve." She could not have imagined on that day that such a call would ever come, but in November of that year, she and her husband Don moved with their two youngest children to Wiesbaden Germany, and her life's greatest story began to unfold.

Germany wasn't their first overseas experience. Don's job as a civilian employee of the Defense Department had taken the Carlsons to Italy and Belgium a decade before. In fact, it was during their years in Belgium that Marianne earned her college degree.

All the travel and the continual moving meant that Marianne was always looking for another job, another foot in the door, another opportunity to expand her skills. In Germany, she was offered a job on the American Army base at Wiesbaden, where she would work as an IT Specialist for the US Army.

"I knew when I took the job", Marianne explains, "that it was a deployable position. But I accepted it for three very good reasons. Number one, I really needed a job, and the Army's policy to grant hiring preference to military spouses had kept me out of work for almost a year. I didn't feel like I was in a position to turn down the first job I'd even interviewed for in 11 months. Secondly, 9-11 was still very fresh in my mind, and I really meant it when I said I'd go anywhere my country asked me to go. But most importantly (in retrospect), I simply couldn't imagine a scenario in which the United States Army would send me – 45 years old, overweight, out of shape, and wholly unskilled in warfare – into any kind deployment situation."

She laughs now and adds, "That just shows you how little I knew about the United States Army."

She accepted the position and 3 months later, in February of 2003, her unit was deployed to Iraq. She joined them in July and spent the next six months providing IT support to the 3rd Corps Support Command in Balad, Iraq.

"It was the most horrible, frightening, disgusting, exhausting, humiliating, difficult thing I have ever been through", she says. "But in many ways, it was the best experience of my life."

Marianne learned some very important things about herself while she was in Iraq. She often tells people, "One thing I learned is that I am way too old to be doing something I hate for a living! But the other thing I learned is that I truly love the United States military. I've met people for whom Duty, Honor, and Country are not just words, and it has been my privilege to call them my friends."

When Don's assignment in Germany ended, they returned to the States, this time moving to New York State, just over an hour from the US Military Academy at West Point. The opportunity for Marianne to work at the Academy was immensely appealing to her, but she vowed she'd never fix another computer as long as she lived. She went to West Point to apply for any job that would get her back to work with the Army. Any job except fixing computers, that is.

Eventually, she got the call for the job that would lead her into web design. It seems that the Chief of Staff of the Army – the highest ranking officer in the Army – had a vision for a project that would be part of the legacy that he would leave behind when he retired. He envisioned an online leadership development tool that would provide guidance and training in leadership skills to Army personnel around the world. When the Department of Behavioral Science and Leadership at West Point was directed to build that tool, they hired Marianne, and eventually she became the web designer for that project.

When her husband retired, they moved to Florida and started Emcie Media, a business that allows her to pursue her passions for web design, writing, and public speaking.

GLOSSARY

artiste   A Commercial Artist, Graphic Designer, or other artist who is highly creative, and often obsessed with his own art.

domain   The spot on the Internet reserved for a specific website or collection of websites.

domain name   A website's name on the Internet. (emcie.com, for example)

e-commerce   The sale of products and services over the Internet. Also, the ability of a website to handle online transactions, accept payments, or manage inventories.

FTP account.   A special account on a hosting server that allows users to upload files in order to update or edit the website.

geek   Once considered a derogatory term, the name is now embraced by most who match its description: a person who is highly skilled in technology, and often obsessed with technical pursuits.

hosting   Service that maintains web servers and permits clients to store their website files on those servers, so that those websites are connected to the World Wide Web.

maintenance   Service that provides updates and re-designs of a website in order to keep its content current, relevant and up-to-date.

PageRank   The patented algorithm, named after Larry Page (a co-founder of Google), which is used by Google to measure the relative importance of various web pages, in relation to each other and to the words entered in the search.   The results of the algorithm are displayed on a SERP.

payment gateway   An e-commerce service that authorizes online credit card payments. It is typically associated with the online store's a merchant account.

results page   The web page that a search engine displays to show the results of a user's search.

search engine   A tool designed to search for information on the Internet.   Google is an example of a search engine.

Search Engine Optimization (SEO)   The science behind improving a website's SERP rank.

SERP   An acronym that stands for Search Engine Results Page which, as the name implies, is the web page that displays the results of a user's search.

SERP rank   The placement of the corresponding link on the SERP, where higher placement means higher SERP rank.

site map   A is a webpage that includes a list of all the webpages on the website.

web server   A computer that provides connectivity to the Internet.

website   A place on the Internet that provides pages of information or entertainment. Also, the component files, data, links, etc, that comprise a website.

wiki   a website that allows its visitors to create and edit its content using any browser.

www.ingramcontent.com/pod-product-compliance
Lightning Source LLC
Chambersburg PA
CBHW051054050326
40690CB00006B/713